Vietnam

A Kick Start Guide
for Business Travelers

Guy & Victoria Brooks

Self-Counsel Press
(*a division of*)
International Self-Counsel Press Ltd.
Canada U.S.A.

Printed in Canada

First edition: February, 1995

Canadian Cataloguing in Publication Data
Brooks, Guy, 1955-
    Vietnam

    (Self-counsel business series)
    ISBN 0-88908-843-8

1. Vietnam — Guidebooks. 2. Vietnam — Economic conditions. 3. Business travel — Vietnam. I. Brooks, Victoria, 1951- II. Title. III. Series.
DS556.25.B76 1995   915.9704'4   C95-910143-8

Self-Counsel Press
(a division of)
International Self-Counsel Press Ltd.

Head and Editorial Office	*U.S. Address*
1481 Charlotte Road	1704 N. State Street
North Vancouver, B.C.	Bellingham, Washington
V7J 1H1	98225

Contents

Maps

Notice to Readers

Every effort is made to keep this publication as current as possible. However, it is the nature of travel books that some information could become outdated between the time of writing and publication. Prices, telephone and fax numbers, addresses, and hours of operations of businesses are subject to change without notice. Readers are asked to take this into account when consulting this guide.

The authors, the publisher, and the vendor of this book make no representations or warranties regarding the outcome or the use to which the information in this book is put and are not assuming any liability for any claims, losses, or damages arising out of the use of this book. The reader should not rely on the authors or publisher of this book for any professional advice.

Introduction

Who Should Read *Vietnam*

This guide was specifically researched and written for the business traveler who has little practical knowledge of Vietnam. It is also for the entrepreneur, always on the lookout for new business opportunities.

A business traveler to Vietnam must cope with energy-sapping heat, culture and language barriers, government red tape, and strange surroundings. Any new proposition is difficult in a country where the standard and quality of life is a far cry from what we are used to. In Vietnam, business travelers may be mystified and shocked by life around them, but they are also usually charmed and caught in Vietnam's embrace. Vietnam is a rewarding experience for people who travel there for any reason.

A definite bonus is the chance to see a country that was closed to the outside world for years. In 1975, North Vietnamese communist forces captured Saigon, reunifying Vietnam after more than 30 years of continuous warfare with France, Japan, and the

United States. From then until February 8, 1994, Vietnam was isolated from the outside world.

Today, as it begins to open its doors, Vietnam seems stuck in a time warp, but that will quickly change. In what other city with a population of 4.5 million would you need to travel in a "cyclo" because there are so few cars available? Only in Vietnam!

Therein lies the fascination that Vietnam holds. Vietnam is a country not just for the entrepreneur, but for the modern adventurer, the curious, the sentimental, and even the lover of culture.

Ho Chi Minh City, or Saigon as the locals still call it, holds in its yellowed palm reminders of both the French colonies and the American presence during the Vietnam war years. It is a fabulous place that once seen, fires your imagination. It is also an Asian-style plum of opportunity waiting to be plucked from the tree.

Vietnam offers almost unbelievable opportunities for entrepreneurial companies or individuals in almost any field, especially manufacturing, importing, exporting, infrastructure services, and, of course, travel and tourism.

You can't open a newspaper without seeing headlines like "Foreign Firms Pour Into Vietnam" or "Investors Follow The Ho Chi Minh Trail." Since President Clinton lifted the embargo against Vietnam on February 8, 1994, a new era has dawned for that country. Vietnam really is one of the world's last frontiers and so it is attracting the attention it deserves.

> **Note of interest:** Saigon hotels are running at a 90% occupancy rate and hoteliers have yet to proclaim an off-season, although this may change with the many renovations and new hotels opening.

Even before the American embargo was lifted, businesses were clamoring to get a foothold in Vietnam, and it's certainly not too late. Vietnam is still changing slowly, and anyone with patience and an eye for opportunity can get in now and be in for the long run. Markets and opportunities will grow for the next few decades as Vietnam comes of age.

Although Vietnam is one of the poorest countries in the world, the possibility of marketing your products to this very new domestic market (Vietnam has a potentially untapped market of over 71 million people) and picking and making new or old products to distribute in your home country can be an exciting reality in Vietnam. The majority (80%) of the population is under 40 and the labor force is hardworking and cheap even by Asian standards. Added to this is Vietnam's treasure trove of natural resources, many as yet untouched and ready for the entrepreneur.

> **Note of interest:** The first North American recording stars to market themselves in concert in Vietnam were rock star Bryan Adams and later, country singer John Denver. Denver drew a crowd of Vietnamese who paid $30 a ticket, which was the average monthly wage of a middle-ranking civil servant at the time.

How to Use *Vietnam*

Our task in writing this guide was to show you, an interested business traveler, how to begin the research and groundwork necessary to do business in Vietnam, while avoiding common but usually unknown pitfalls. This book tells you what you need to know to make your trip comfortable and interesting. We also sincerely hope it will give you an appreciation of the country and help you answer the question: Do you really want to do business or spend time there?

Vietnam outlines concisely and in an interesting, sometimes personal manner, cultural idiosyncrasies that you need to know to be effective in business dealings. The result will be an easier adjustment for you, which means your mind can focus on business matters, not overcoming culture shock!

The groundwork and information will be of general interest to anyone on a first-time business mission to Vietnam. You will learn where to get the best rate of exchange, how to leave the airport in the most expedient manner, and the best means of getting around. Just as important, the book shows you how to quickly and comfortably set up the all-important initial visit.

Entrepreneurial tips provide suggestions on many sectors of business, including infrastructure, natural resources, manufacturing, and a special section on tourism and financial services. Some interesting buying opportunities for art and crafts have also been noted.

We've also included special notes of interest: anecdotes or issues designed to help you appreciate what goes on in these countries. Skip them if your time is limited!

How This Book Came About

We wrote this book together, with much help both in the research and writing from our son, Tyson, while doing a business fact-finding mission in Vietnam. We immediately saw the need for a guide like this while we were doing research for the trip. The only books available were travel guides, culture shock books, and business books that used too many statistics and graphs and had little to do with getting business done. They were useful for compiling statistics and getting addresses, but did nothing to help prepare for getting an appointment with managing directors, learning the correct business etiquette, or getting the best value for your money.

The first time we arrived in Vietnam, we were surrounded by touts wanting to drive us to our hotel. It was only after much confusion and some luck that we found out what the proper fare was. Another traveler had paid five times the proper taxi fare and was subjected to a non-air-conditioned, filthy, smoke-filled car that masqueraded as a taxi.

Being hardened travelers, we had researched and meticulously booked our hotel room in advance. But when we were escorted to our expensive, five-star hotel room, there was only one double bed and no room for a third bed for our son, Tyson, let alone for his then 5' 10" body on the floor. When we notified the desk, we were told that this was the only style room the hotel offered. Extra beds were not and never had been available. It didn't matter that we had requested a third bed when we had booked.

We were lucky we hadn't arrived in the middle of the night, but we still had to collect our luggage and start again. If we hadn't researched beforehand, we would not have even known the name of a suitable hotel to go to. We can't guarantee that something like this won't ever happen to you, but with this book the chances are dramatically reduced.

Vietnam does not and is not meant to replace specific business books that use statistics and lists (e.g.,

Vietnam Investment Review, published by the Vietnam government), but it supplements them with the practical information a businessperson needs in order to get through the preparation and first days of a business trip without having a mini-breakdown.

We've done your walking for you, so you can kick start yourself into action as soon as you land.

1 Vietnam — The Land and the People

Vietnam is one of the last strongholds of communism — more properly now, socialism — but its style has changed and is still changing. In 1977, Vietnam took steps to change its laws in an effort to attract foreign investment. In 1986, the communist government made a decision to move toward a free market economy. In 1992, Vietnam did something that we westerners are fortunate to take for granted. It amended its constitution so that for the first time the Party (meaning the government), had to operate within the law of the land.

> **Tip:** Be aware that "the law of the land" can and does change. Make sure every step you take is a careful and documented one.

Vietnam Positives

"The Sleeping Tiger" and "Sweetheart of the Future" are nicknames given to Vietnam for its huge financial potential. Investors are flocking there! Between 1991 and 1994, the economy has grown by 7% a year. Target figures for the future show 8% and over. As well, inflation has been reduced from a double digit figure to 9%, and the Vietnamese government is committed to a market economy.

The economy is getting a boost from a wave of foreign investment that is helping to rebuild Vietnam's weak, physical infrastructure and revitalize its legal and administrative framework. In 1994, eight foreign banks, including the Bank of America, loaned Vietnam U.S. $100 million to upgrade infrastructure.

In order to control the traffic, Hanoi plans to spend U.S. $8.5 billion to build an elevated railway and expand roads and bus routes by the middle of the twenty-first century. It is expected that Hanoi will double its paved surface area.

Other recent changes include a guarantee that foreign enterprises will not be nationalized and a commitment to a liberal foreign investment policy. By taking these kinds of steps, the communist government is making the country attractive to the outside world.

Tip: The Asian Development Bank predicts that Vietnam will be the leader in economic growth in Southeast Asia, with over 8% growth. This puts Vietnam ahead of Thailand, Indonesia, and Malaysia.

Vietnam Negatives

Vietnam is poor by any standard. The average annual income is around U.S. $200, although this hasn't stopped Coca Cola, Singer, and many other large companies from marketing their products to the Vietnamese.

Corruption is not unusual in Southeast Asia, but Vietnam has a reputation for being one of the worst offenders. Even though in 1988, after reforms were made, over 1,000 officials were prosecuted for corruption, the problem hasn't gone away.

Just one example is the case of Legamex, the textiles company that was to be the flagship of Vietnam's privatization program. In 1994, it was rocked by a new corruption scandal. Charges of company money being used to help friends' businesses and directing share allocations to relatives were made. Subsequently, heads rolled and the sale of Legamex shares to the public was suspended.

Word has it that to get a contract with the local government in the southern part of the country, a bribe or "commission" of 15% has to be paid. This percentage has escalated with time.

A spokesperson for the People's Committee blames the corruption on the move to a market economy, which has encouraged greed and the pursuit of profit. Whether or not this is true, Vietnam is committed to privatization. Unfortunately, the government's bid to curb corruption has resulted in even more red tape than before, which is one of the biggest complaints of people trying to do business there.

Add to this the complication of the continually changing rules and regulations because of the newness of the market economy. Each time the government changes the rules, there exists the potential for confusion.

Despite these problems, foreign investment is still booming, exports are still growing, and inflation is under control. The problem of corruption seems more like an annoying thorn in the side of Vietnam's winning combination of dynamism, stability, and potential.

History

To understand Vietnam, you have to take at least a brief look at its past. The years of dominance and invasion by various foreign powers and the long struggle for independence and the search for cultural and national identity has affected the Vietnamese character and made the people resilient, independent, and above all, optimistic.

Early Occupation

The Chinese occupied Vietnam from A.D. 207 to A.D. 938. The roots of Buddhism, Confucianism, Taoism, and feudalism stem from the Chinese presence.

After the occupation, feudal dynasties ruled. During this time, the kingdom of Vietnam spread to what is now Cambodia and Laos. Even during this period of independence, Vietnam was busy repelling attacks by the Mongolians and Chinese. They also suffered through civil wars.

Modern-day foreign interference began in the early seventeenth century when France came to assist Vietnam in one of its civil uprisings and French missionaries set out to convert the Vietnamese to Catholicism.

In 1862, the new French colony of Cochinchina was established by force over the Vietnamese. The French colonists taxed the peasantry into poverty and expropriated land. Both these factors contributed to the breakdown of the land ownership system that was central to Vietnamese social tradition.

The displaced rural Vietnamese were left in poverty. Some were forced to live a nomadic lifestyle, roaming the countryside looking for work. Others settled in the infertile highlands and made a meager living by slash-and-burn farming. The majority were indentured as plantation and mining laborers. Thousands died from malnutrition and disease. Ironically, it is the French-influenced architecture, especially in Saigon, that contributes to the charm that Vietnam now holds.

The Vietnamese didn't welcome their colonial masters. Strong Vietnamese nationalism led to sporadic violence and confrontations with the French. Between 1925 and 1941, a peasant-based movement led by Ho Chi Minh crystallized. Eventually, this group would be known as the Viet Minh, the Viet Cong, and still later as the Vietnamese Communist Party.

In World War II, the Japanese displaced the French and occupied Vietnam for six months before the bombing of Hiroshima and Nagasaki. At the 1945 Potsdam Conference, it was agreed that the Chinese Kuomintang would accept the Japanese surrender north of the 16th parallel and the British would do the same in the south. This proved to be a disaster. When the British arrived to accept the surrender of the Japanese, the Vietnamese factions were on the brink of civil war, and the French settlers were taking the law into their own hands. In an attempt to restore order, the British asked the defeated Japanese for help. They also released and armed 1,400 French paratroopers who had been imprisoned in 1945 for plotting to overthrow the then-occupying Japanese army. These French paratroopers went on a violent rampage, overthrew the government in the south, and violently and indiscriminately beat Vietnamese men, women, and children in their homes. Meanwhile in the north, the Chinese were pillaging their way to Hanoi.

Once the war ended, Ho Chi Minh seized the opportunity and, in the August Revolution, took control of North and Central Vietnam, declaring it the New Republic of Vietnam. Thus began the post-war independence struggle (First Indochinese War) that lasted for eight years against the French. In its wake came the Second Indochinese or Vietnam War against the United States.

The Vietnam War

In 1954, at the Geneva Accords, a provisional line at the 17th parallel divided Vietnam until political settlement could be achieved by nationwide elections. This division of the country into North Vietnam and South Vietnam placed the south under a government ruled by Ngo Dinh Diem. Diem was a fervent Catholic and anti-communist. (His brother had been killed by the Viet Minh in 1945.)

Ho Chi Minh's North Vietnam government was given control of the territory north of the 17th parallel. Immediately, he took repressive measures against anything that threatened Hanoi's power. Ten thousand Vietnamese were executed and 50,000 to 100,000 imprisoned, many without trial. A radical land reform act was also implemented. This, plus the American fear of the spread of communism in areas where the United States had political and economic interests, resulted in the American backing of President Diem's South Vietnam and the ensuing Vietnam War.

The U.S. military presence in Vietnam began in the early 1960s. By 1970, both antiwar sentiment by the American public and war casualties reached a peak. And finally, in 1973, President Richard Nixon called for the withdrawal of all armed forces personnel and the return of prisoners of war. During the war years, 58,000 Americans were killed or missing in action. Hundreds of thousands of North Vietnamese and 223,748 South Vietnamese soldiers were killed. As well, statistics say 10% of the Vietnamese population or four million civilians lost their lives. Approximately 300,000 Vietnamese and 1,800 Americans are still listed as missing in action.

Aftermath of the War

On April 30, 1975, Ho Chi Minh's Communists took Saigon, and the south fell to the Communist north. Shortly afterwards, Vietnam was reunified, and on July 2, 1976, the formation of the Socialist Republic of Vietnam was declared. The post-war government was faced with the daunting task of rebuilding the economy, consolidating power, and solving social problems like prostitution, illiteracy, criminal activity, and homelessness.

Hanoi wanted a quick transition to socialism for the south, including agricultural collectivism. Reunification was set up as a socialist system based on the Soviet model. This proved difficult for the south, because it had functioned as a capitalist society until then. Private enterprises were shut down, and control of remaining businesses was given to northern military personnel. The result was widespread economic mismanagement.

Hundreds of thousands of south Vietnamese were thrown into labor camps (re-education camps) without trial. Catholic, Protestant, and Buddhist religious leaders, intellectuals, union leaders, journalists, and anyone who had ties to the former regime ended up doing forced labor. The end result of this repression led to an exodus of close to a million Vietnamese.

Some escaped by boat, others by fleeing overland through Cambodia.

Vietnam's slow economic comeback and journey back into the outside world began in May, 1977, when U.S. opposition to Vietnamese membership in the United Nations was dropped. Vietnam then became the 149th member of the UN.

But progress stopped when differences arose between the United States and Vietnam, including the demand from the Vietnamese for billions of dollars in reparations. Only a year later, China cut off all aid to Vietnam, and in 1979, China invaded the north. This move was believed to be in retaliation for the age-old antipathy of the Vietnamese toward the Chinese.

As well, in late 1978, after two years of Cambodian attacks on the Vietnamese border villages by the communist Khmer Rouge, Vietnam invaded Cambodia. The Vietnamese successfully drove Pol Pot's murderous Khmer Rouge from power with support from the Soviets. (The Khmer Rouge backed by China had taken over Cambodia in 1975.) They installed their own pro-Hanoi leader, a former Khmer Rouge, as President. As a result, the United States severed all ties with Vietnam and convinced its western allies to impose an aid embargo.

That embargo lasted until 1994 when President Bill Clinton finally ended it. Meanwhile, Vietnam had withdrawn from Cambodia in 1989, fulfilling part of the conditions for normalization of relations with the western world.

The termination of foreign relations, the drain on resources from the occupation of Cambodia, and the mismanagement by the socialist government over the years contributed to Vietnam's severe economic trouble.

Country Profile

Area

This S-shaped country is 331,685 square km (132,674 square mi.), which makes it smaller than the State of Washington. Vietnam also claims a series of islands extending from the Gulf of Tonkin to the Gulf of Thailand.

The Red and the Mekong rivers, which are the richest rivers in the region (in terms of marine life), both flow through the country. The Mekong winds down from the highlands in Tibet to the South China Sea.

Vietnamese topography varies from mountains to jungles to grassy plains.

Location

Vietnam is bordered strategically by the South China Sea on the east and the south, with a coastline stretching 3,000 km (1,865 mi.). China sits on the north, and Laos and Cambodia on the west. Vietnam's two biggest rice bowls are located in the Red River delta and the Mekong delta. The city of Saigon is located in the south and Hanoi is the north.

> **Note of interest:** Vietnamese describe their country as a bamboo pole with a bucket of rice at each end. The pole is the long slim part of Vietnam characterized by mountain ranges. The rice buckets are the Mekong River delta area of the south and the Red River Delta in the north.

Divisions

Vietnam is divided into 40 provinces. Hanoi, Haiphong, and Ho Chi Minh City are designated as municipalities. Vietnamese cities are divided into areas called "quartiers" or "quan."

Population

The population of Vietnam is 71 million, with a density of 210 people per square km (130 people per square mi.), making it the 12th most populated country on earth. Urban areas make up 20% of the population, with Ho Chi Minh City and Hanoi accounting for half this figure. According to the United Nations Development Program, 80% of the population is under the age of 40.

The capital city of Hanoi has three million people, but the largest city is Saigon with 4.5 million. Haiphong has a population of 1.5 million and the coastal city of Da Nang has half a million people.

Population growth is one of the biggest problems facing the development of Vietnam. The growth rate is one of the top ten in the world and is set at 2.1%. About 70,000 new babies are born in Saigon each year. Medical facilities are in short supply and of low standard.

A population control campaign called "two is enough," has been launched by the government. Free contraceptives and incentives for sterilization and vasectomies are offered. The goal is a birth rate of 1.1% in the next decade.

People

The majority of the population is ethnic Vietnamese or Viet.

Vietnam has 53 ethnic minority groups that make up 11% of the population.

Of the several ethnic groups the Kinh is the largest. Other important groups are the Thai (one million) and ethnic Chinese (one million). The Chinese live mainly in Cholon, Saigon's sister city.

There are also various indigenous hill tribes, mostly mountain people or "montagnards." They are semi-nomadic, and often exist outside government control. Recent market reform has led the montagnards to grow opium as a cash crop. Up until now they only grew enough for personal use.

When trying to understand the Vietnamese people, you must appreciate the differences between the north and the south. When communist forces took over Saigon in April, 1975, they ended over a century of division between north and south Vietnam.

There are definite marked economic, social, and political differences between the people of the north and the south. It can be argued that northerners have more Chinese and Confucianist traits, whereas southerners are more open and direct, less conservative, and not as thrifty as northerners.

These differences are easy to understand when you consider Vietnam's history. Foreign involvement in the south plus better living conditions head the list. The north suffers because its climate is harsher, including typhoons and wet, cold winters, while the south has a tropical climate. This makes it harder to make a living in the north. There is also a larger population in the north and this has lead to land shortages.

One theory attributes the north/south personality difference to Vietnam's history of migration and assimilation. By the fifteenth century, landless peasants, criminals, and political exiles were forced south to central Vietnam. There they soon conquered the Cham empire. Later they moved further south to the Mekong delta and displaced the Khmer or Cambodians. They had picked up cultural traits from the Cham and the Khmer who had assimilated Indian cultural traits.

Geographical location and western influence add to this theory. Hanoi has no seaport, so it was closed to outside influences other than China, while the south is more open to Southeast Asia. Southern influence was intensified when the French came. France colonized the south and kept central and north Vietnam as protectorates. When the French were defeated in 1954, Vietnam became a symbol of the struggle between communism and capitalism, the south taking on the presence and influence of the United States and the western world, while the north lived the communist way.

The standard of living, per capita income, desire for democracy, and adjustment to market reform is much higher in the south, making it easier to do business there. The south produces over one-half of Vietnam's gross domestic product, but has less than one-third the population. Ho Chi Minh City, popularly known as Saigon, is the center of economic development.

Religion

The religion of Vietnam is predominantly Buddhism, but also Confucianism and animism. Vietnamese would readily admit that their religion is a mix of the three beliefs.

Buddhism was introduced into Vietnam first by dissident Chinese monks who took refuge in Vietnam. This is known as Northern Buddhism. Later, in the third century, Buddhist monks from India settled in Vietnam, and this branch of the religion is known as Southern Buddhism. Although no statistics are available, it is believed that the majority of the south is Buddhist.

Simply put, Buddhism stresses the law of Karma. This is a record of good and bad deeds that must balance out on the side of good or your next life will be worse. After many lives, each better than the rest, one can enter Nirvana, or a state of oneness with the universe. Only then can the cycle end.

Confucianism was introduced into Vietnam at the beginning of Chinese domination, which lasted for almost 1,000 years. Confucianism is not a true religion, but a code of ethics. It teaches that humans are essentially good, can distinguish between good and evil, and if we live a virtuous life, will receive tranquility of the soul.

Confucianism is based on a code of ethics that stresses harmony of relationships. Ancestor worship is an important ritual and must be observed in order to obtain tranquility of the spiritual soul. At death the living soul turns to dust along with the body, but the spiritual soul can remain alive. When a person dies, the soul becomes the protector of the family. The living have a duty to their ancestors to keep the spiritual soul alive and protect it through ancestor worship.

Ancestor worship is practiced during festivals and holidays, plus in the home. An altar decorated with pictures of the dead person, incense, flowers, candles, and the names of the dead is kept in the house.

Animism is the belief that all natural objects and the universe itself possess a soul. Animism is deeply ingrained in the Vietnamese, especially in the peasant population. The communist authorities have tried to suppress animism, although the constitution guarantees religious freedom.

> **Note of interest:** Spiritism, superstition, and fortune telling are important to the Vietnamese. For example, a mirror on a front door is meant to trick a dragon into thinking that there is another dragon there. Then the dragon will not enter the house.

Politics

Vietnam is a socialist republic. The 1.8 million member Communist Party (Dang Cong San Vietnam) was founded in 1930 by Ho Chi Minh. It is flexible by communist standards.

The most powerful arm of the Party is the Politburo. Its dozen members oversee daily functions and have the power to make directives to the government.

Because the structure of the Party is decentralized, local leaders are allowed to take their own initiative. In recent years, the Party has made progressive reforms for economic renovation (*doi moi*).

The Party leads both the state and all classes of society according to Ho Chi Minh and Marxist-Leninist doctrines. Party organizations work within a framework established by both the country's laws and the constitution.

A new constitution was adopted by the National Assembly in April, 1992, making the Communist Party subject to the laws of the state and the constitution. Through its new constitution, Vietnam is defined as a state "of the people, by the people, and for the people." Power is exercised through the National Assembly and local People's Councils under the principle of "democratic centralism."

Vietnamese citizens have recently been granted rights that give them freedom of movement and residence within the country, and freedom of passage both in and out of Vietnam. Citizens were also recently granted the rights to ownership of lawful income, savings, houses, private enterprises, and capital and other assets required for private enterprise. The constitution also made reforms to encourage foreign investment. The economy's reform program, *doi moi*, calls for "a multi-sector commodity economy operating in a market-oriented system, under the control of the state and in accordance with socialist ideals."

The National Assembly is the highest governing body and has 395 members (*Quoc Hoi*) and meets twice every year. The Council of State is a legislative body appointed by the National Assembly. It has the power to pass ordinances when the National Assembly is in recess. Elections take place every five years.

The head of state is the Chairman of the Council of the state. The Council is responsible to and appointed by the National Assembly and it can issue decrees for the implementation of ordinances and laws consistent with existing legislation. If there is no law, the Council of Ministers can issue decrees until superseded by legal ordinance.

The Standing Committee of the Council of Ministers is the executive arm. It has authority in special areas of responsibility: the State Committee for Cooperation and Investment (SCCI), the State Committee for Inspection, the State Committee for Prices, the State Committee for Planning, the State Committee for Science, and the State Bank.

> **Note of interest:** Petrovietnam has special ministerial status similar to the Standing Committees.

Local government comprises centrally controlled provinces and municipalities divided into towns, districts, and villages. Each city has a People's Committee, which has authority over its area and is elected locally.

The Supreme Court is the ultimate legal authority with regional, military, and people's courts acting as subordinate courts. In December, 1993, new economic courts were sanctioned by the National Assembly to deal with investment issues.

Questions for the Future

Both the government and foreign businesspeople worry that a backlash against corruption could turn the people against the government or provide a cover for hard-liners in the communist government who oppose privatization and decentralization.

The Vietnamese have a long-term vision for their hard-won independence, and worry that now that the gates are finally open, there will be no gatekeepers.

For three decades, Vietnam's government concentrated on waging war. No time or money was left for education or economic management. Some Vietnamese criticize the government for its lack of knowledge about the free market economy, including management techniques. The government wants to encourage foreign investment, but it also wants to protect people from exploitation at the hands of unscrupulous businesspeople. This is a moral concern for anyone who deals with Vietnam.

2 Opening the Door — and Keeping It Open

Back in 1986, Vietnam realized it needed foreign investment and began to liberalize its economy. It recognized that its wars, history of international isolation, and poor state planning had left it economically weak. Economists at the time said that the Vietnamese foreign investment code was one of the most liberal anywhere. Even so, investors didn't flock to invest in Vietnam. One reason was the U.S. economic embargo; the other was that there was no commercial law to protect the investor. It didn't help that there was no decent infrastructure, including airports or even hotels.

But these barriers have all been removed. President Clinton lifted the embargo, commercial laws regarding foreign investment are now being addressed by the Vietnamese government, and the infrastructure has improved to the point that stylish restaurants and five-star hotels are available in Saigon. (In fact, the need to further improve the infrastructure presents a giant opportunity for the entrepreneur.)

Preparation

It is very important to realize that even when you are doing something very simple, like buying a container-erful of laquerware or rattan furniture, you may need a Vietnamese to assist you in setting it up. Government permission is needed for everything — export permits are required for the simplest things — and without a savvy Vietnamese partner, you may go home in frustration.

Tip: The Vietnamese Chamber of Commerce and Industry publishes a business directory aimed at helping you find a business partner in Vietnam. There are classifications for all industries. At the time of writing, the price was U.S. $140 and you can pay by Visa or MasterCard. You can write and request it from —
PC Book Centre Pte Ltd.
865 Mountbatten Road #02-55
Katong Shopping Centre, Singapore 1543
Tel: (65)447 1557
Fax: (65)447 0791

If this is your first trip to confirm the market size and potential for your particular interest, it is advisable to establish a contact in a local law firm and an accounting firm. Your own lawyer and accountant at home may have offices or affiliate offices in Vietnam, so always check first. If they don't, ask your lawyer to find you a firm and give you an introduction. Most law firms in Vietnam will give you an initial interview for free.

A reputable law firm is indispensable. They will help you identify opportunities and will act as a liaison for your contacts in both the government and the private sector. Call your Vietnamese consulate, who will put you in touch with a reputable local firm. After the initial interview, your representative will work on a contract basis. Ask about charges before local representatives begin any work on your behalf.

If you have no contacts in Vietnam, locate firms in your home city that may be able to provide you with the names of associates or firms. Embassies, trade commissions, and relevant associations for your industry will also be happy to refer you and give you contacts.

Note: If you are already hot on the trail of a joint venture and know what you want, be sure to make an appointment before you arrive in Vietnam with The Peoples Committee of Saigon at City Hall. There are legal requirements for doing everything. If you get caught without permission from the applicable government agency, you will be thrown out of the country and risk losing what you have already invested. Every government ministry has a consulting department or company and they will consult for a fee.

Tip: We can personally recommend Chor Pee & Company. In 1993, they extended their practice beyond Singapore and Malaysia and opened offices in Saigon and Hanoi. They are very helpful, knowledgeable, and positive people who can take you all the way through a business deal. In Saigon, the firm's address is —

The Colonade
27 Nguyen Trung Truc
District 1
Ho Chi Minh City, Vietnam
Tel: (848)224986
Fax: (848)225441.

In Hanoi, the address is —

43 D Ngo Quyen Street
Hoan Kiem District, Hanoi
Vietnam
Tel: (844)251213
Fax: (844)251875

Business in Vietnam is done face-to-face — personal contact is vital — so don't be disappointed if your initial letters and fax are not answered. A personal phone call and later a visit will ensure the beginnings of a relationship.

Letters of Introduction

You will want to obtain a letter of introduction which you can either bring with you or have your local law/accounting firm fax to its Vietnamese contact. If the letter is faxed for you, be sure your objective and arrival date are clearly stated.

The local Vietnamese firms receive many such requests and are happy to spend an hour or so discussing the local scene. Of course, they hope you will actually commence your project and use them to represent you.

Gather all the information and introductions you can. People doing business in Vietnam can find a lot in common and will go out of their way to give you their introductions.

> **Tip:** Business titles are very important when doing business in Asia. If you have a title or any designation, don't forget to include it in your letter of introduction.

Appointments and Contacts

If your time is short or you believe your contact to be very busy, it is advisable to fax ahead confirming when you will be telephoning to make an appointment.

Suggest two possible dates to ensure you'll get an appointment.

Don't forget to refer in your fax to your local contact or attach a letter of introduction from your contact.

You may prefer to visit your Vietnamese contact *after* you have familiarized yourself with local conditions, including market appraisal. You will then be educated enough to maximize your visit.

Tip: Get further relevant referrals from each appointment. Most people, including foreigners in Vietnam, love to network and welcome friends of friends or even acquaintances. Obviously if they think they'll get some business, they will also welcome you with open arms.

Always keep in mind that you need help doing business in Vietnam; you are allowed *nothing* unless you go through proper government channels. Any private contact you can make with someone who knows the ropes can streamline your route to success.

The Etiquette of Business

It is of utmost importance in business and on social occasions to respect, follow, and be aware of tradition, religion, and customs with the Vietnamese. This includes being aware of their history and the cultural differences between north and south.

Vietnamese culture has been based on agriculture, mostly wet rice farming. This calls for people to be in close contact with each other and to be mutually dependent. It is ingrained in the Vietnamese to value harmony, modesty, and to strive for the family, the village, the nation, and not for the individual. Added to these values have been the communist or socialist ethic and Confucianism.

The differences between the north and south make it more difficult for foreigners doing business. Government people are typically northerners. Keep that in mind when you are dealing with government officials. As well, because the Chinese spent so much time in Vietnam, some common traits are held by both races. Remember the Chinese reputation for being astute, tough businesspeople. The Vietnamese are no different. Anyone who has negotiated with the Vietnamese knows that you cannot pull the wool over their eyes!

Tip: The northerners have kept more Chinese traits than their southern cousins. But although the Vietnamese have definite Chinese traits, they do not get along. Do not remind a Vietnamese that he or she is like a Chinese person.

You will meet two distinctly different types of businesspeople in Vietnam. The first is the person who signs your permits — the government "party man" from

Hanoi. He is not likely to be an expert in your field, an expert in management, or even the boss. However, he is the one who decides whether your project falls within party policy. If he decides in your favor, he will be the person who will help you get the government approvals you need.

The second type of person is not affiliated with the government. The government is finally accepting that it needs non-party talent if it is to succeed in its market reform. These important businesspeople, who could end up being your joint venture partners, are often southern Vietnamese who were trained under the old regime. Remember the differences when dealing with north and south.

Tip: Corruption and bureaucracy are facts of life. Help smooth your path by having a Vietnamese friend in middle management. He or she can help make sure your permits are put on the right government official's desk rather than languishing in dust, mildew, and the stickiest of red tape. Remember that you need written permission for almost everything. Use a law firm based in Vietnam that has many years' experience doing business there and dealing with government.

Communication Gaps

The differences between eastern and western social values can cause much misunderstanding. The Asian method of stressing calmness and harmonious relationships can be interpreted as "beating around the bush" by westerners, who are generally more assertive.

Out of politeness to avoid confrontation, or because of a misunderstanding, a Vietnamese will sometimes seem to agree while having no intention of doing so. He or she may also refrain from making direct eye contact. But again, this is done out of politeness, and does not imply a shifty character.

A Vietnamese will either ignore or talk around a perceived problem and hope you will catch the meaning. He or she will not directly confront you. Neither silence or a smile from a Vietnamese can be interpreted as agreement. In Vietnam, a smile can also indicate embarrassment, anger, or frustration.

Tip: Since many Vietnamese do not speak English, you will need a translator. Either bring your own — someone you trust — or politely and expediently test the one in question. Many pretend to understand but don't!

Many first-time business travelers from the west go home excited about the potential and think a particular deal is closer to completion than it is. Verbally confirm your discussions and negotiations as well as the other party's understanding of what you are discussing. Be simple, but not simplistic: don't patronize. If possible, get a second confirmation from the same company.

Like most people, Vietnamese — especially government officials — don't like criticism. Be very careful not to make your business contacts think they are losing face. This could cost you the deal!

Etiquette and Understanding

Vietnamese value self-control and harmony. They hide their negative feelings and are always mild-mannered and polite. Their need to please makes them agree to things they have no intention of coming through with. Watch out and beware!

If you become aggressive or antagonistic, you will have lost face and their respect. The basic rule for your behavior in Vietnam is never to show anger or annoyance. If you feel you must criticize, it is more acceptable to veil your criticism with a joke and a smile.

Always listen and structure you questions carefully — preferably in a positive way. If you ask a negative question, for example, "You haven't got around to translating that document yet, have you?", the answer you get will be "Yes, I haven't." This can create confusion, so be careful.

Being on Time

Vietnamese are not often late, but you must always be on time. If there is a delay, simply chat with the secretary while you wait and try not to show any agitation. Keep in mind that business meetings can drag on and on, so give yourself a lot of time between appointments.

Vietnamese businesspeople and officials are not usually as anxious or as timely at getting a deal moving as a westerner is. Display patience and tenacity. To keep things moving as fast as possible, make sure you are dealing with the person who has the authority to do what you need. Referrals and previous initial contacts will also help get you attention and a timely response in both the public and private sector.

> **Note of interest:** The Vietnamese write dates in the European style, with the day before the month. For example, February 14, 1995 would be written 14/2/95.

Using Names and Titles

When you see a full Vietnamese name written down, you will see first the surname, then the middle name, and then the given name. For example, in Nguyen Quang Thiep, Nguyen is the surname, Quang the middle name, and Theip the given name. In Vietnam they would call this man Mr. Thiep even though Thiep is his first name. People are always addressed by their given names and always with Mister, Madame (not Mrs.), or Miss before the name. This system works well for the Vietnamese, as the Vietnamese have very few surnames. (The surname Nguyen accounts for half the surnames in Vietnamese.)

Hierarchy and Status

As in most Asian cultures, status, age, and position are important in Vietnam. There is no jealousy, only a positive acceptance.

A foreigner is initially looked upon as being of lower hierarchy, and Vietnamese prefer to be properly introduced before getting to know you. This is the traditional way of establishing trust and respect. It means little except that as a foreigner you will have to take on the Vietnamese qualities of patience and politeness. Remember everything takes a little longer. After the introduction is a good time to give a well-thought-out gift.

Business Cards and Greetings

Business cards are often called name cards. They are very important, so always carry a large supply.

Make sure your business card presents you in the highest possible position because the Vietnamese are impressed by hierarchy and titles and naturally prefer to do business with important people.

Unlike other Asian countries, it is not necessary to present your card with both hands and a bow.

Exchanging cards must be done during verbal introductions and at the beginning of business meetings. Give them to everyone who might be helpful to you.

Tip: If you run out of business cards and want more, you can have high-quality cards made up at the amazing cost of under U.S. $10 for 100 cards. They can be printed on both sides in a minimum of three days, maximum one week. The size is a little bit smaller lengthwise than North American cards. Ask your cyclo driver to take you to Printing House #2 at 6 Mac Thi Buoi in downtown Saigon. Take the stairs, but first notice the fascinating, old printing equipment on the main floor. The equipment may look ancient, but it certainly does the job well.

The modern Vietnamese usually follows the western tradition of shaking hands as a means of introduction. Follow your hosts' example and use the traditional greeting if they do. (Slight bow, with your hands pressed together.)

Women play an important role in business in Vietnam, but they do not traditionally shake hands with men or with other women. Only shake hands with a woman if she offers you her hand first.

The Business Meeting

When you phone to make an appointment for a business meeting, ask for one hour of their time. Business meetings in Vietnam are relatively informal and polite, but they can be long. Leave time for discussion of the issue at the end of the meeting. Close the meeting at the end of your hour.

Once you have shaken hands and exchanged business cards, you can sit down — but not before the senior Vietnamese member has done so. If you are not alone, perhaps accompanied by your colleagues, select a leader who will do the introductions and direct the conversation. Your leader should state the reason for the meeting and then the agenda. He or she should be direct, but not overly firm.

In government meetings, you can expect to be received by a group of high officials including an interpreter and one or two secretaries making notes. Government meetings usually begin with a long speech, so having an agenda of business is crucial if you want to get anywhere. There will always be more than one meeting.

In government meetings especially, do not interrupt. Let your Vietnamese counterpart finish his or her speech before you deal with anything said. Make notes and pose your questions when it is your turn to speak.

> **Tip:** Bring your own interpreter. Everything is translated literally and misinterpretations can occur. When using your interpreter, face the person you are addressing. Do not use third-person pronouns. Be attentive to the speaker, not the interpreter.

It is likely you'll be offered tea and cigarettes. Cigarettes can be politely turned down, but you must take tea. Wait until your hosts have picked up their cups before you pick up yours. If you don't finish the tea, don't worry.

Body Etiquette

Etiquette in Vietnam is a lot less complicated than many Asian countries, but there are still many things to keep in mind.

- Do not kiss anyone except for a child. Public displays of affection are not acceptable. Modesty is important.

- Never touch anyone on the head, including a child, because the head is the spiritual center for the body.

- Many Vietnamese are Buddhist; don't point the soles of your feet at anyone or at any religious figure.

- It is rude to beckon to another person by waving your hand or finger with the palm upright.

- In Vietnam, the gesture for "come here" is the western gesture that means "go away." A Vietnamese person will gesture arm extended, palm angled down, and hand and fingers together, waving when they want you to approach them. It means "come and sit with me."

- Loud boisterous behavior, arguing, and showing public affection to the opposite sex is considered distasteful.

- Standing with your hands folded in front of you denotes respect and reverence in Vietnam, whereas in the western world this signifies aggression, anger, or disinterest.

If you make these small mistakes, you will not be chastised and you will be quickly forgiven. The natural generosity and goodwill of the Vietnamese always ensures this.

Social Taboos

- Always remove your shoes before entering the house of a Vietnamese. You will be offered slippers.

- If you eat with chopsticks, do not leave them sitting vertically in your bowl. Put them beside the bowl on the table.

- Do not wear shorts. Dress in proper business attire. (This applies to men and women.)

- Do not wear white during the Tet holidays (see the Tip given below)

- White, rather than black, is the color worn at funerals.

- Do not discuss any aspect of Vietnam's politics unless you know your host very well.

Tip: Check for Vietnamese holidays, especially Tet before making your flight arrangements. Tet, the Lunar New Year, is the most important holiday of the year. People plan business activities around the various holidays and celebrations. Business doesn't go back to normal until the sixth day after Tet begins.

The Correct Attitude

Vietnamese value trust and prefer to begin business arrangements with personal, relaxed conversations to see what type of person they are dealing with. They will often begin a conversation with a polite query about your family. Some polite chitchat (not about politics or complaints) before you get down to business helps develop a healthy relationship. Compromise, not aggression, is a key to business relations.

Vietnamese are Asians, and no Asian wants to lose face. Don't be aggressive or argumentative: you will embarrass them and show yourself in a bad light. Don't become annoyed over delays, including delays caused by red tape. Negotiations will slow down or break down if you show anger.

> **Tip:** We can't emphasize enough how important contacts are to the Vietnamese. Proper introductions are the key to success.

Negotiations

Make the mental effort of putting yourself in the shoes of the Vietnamese when negotiating. Understand where they are coming from and above all remain reasonable and flexible. Keep these points in mind.

- Although bribes are against the law, gifts for favors are accepted and appreciated.
- A good local consultant who speaks your language and with whom you have built a healthy rapport goes a long way when negotiating in Vietnam.
- Make sure you have a good interpreter when negotiating. Words mean different things in different countries. We know of one case when a deal was being done between a Vietnam company and a Singapore company when different interpretations got in the way. The Singapore company faxed some legal documents to Vietnam. The Vietnamese company didn't understand the word "defendant" and thought they were being sued. In Vietnamese, defendant translates as "accused."
- Try to politely keep communications with government officials to the point. Don't waste time on frivolous matters.

- "Guanxi" — the establishment of a relationship — is important.
- Some Vietnamese have a short-term outlook where making money is concerned. This obviously relates to their past history of poverty. Be careful!

Gifts

Vietnamese in all walks of life give gifts and appreciate receiving them. Presenting a gift at your initial introduction will help ensure your success in future negotiations.

Tip: The Vietnamese tend to be conscious of the status of different brands. A bottle of a name-brand liqueur, especially Scotch, whiskey, or cognac could be just the gift. Johnny Walker is always appreciated. If you give a cheap brand, you might lose face! A carton of cigarettes is also an appreciated gift. Marlboro or 555 are favorites.

If you buy a gift of liquor, be careful. Liquor taxes are high in Vietnam, and liquor sold in the black market costs the same as duty free. Check carefully that the bottles have not been opened and the labels are real. There are two wine and liquor import stores of note in Saigon: La Cave at 54 Le Thanh Ton and La Maison Du Vin at 76 Ngo Duo Ke Street.

Entertaining

Vietnamese men love to entertain, especially in restaurants. These social occasions are important to establish trust and a friendly relationship. Drinking liquor, especially beer, is part of the rite, as is smoking. Don't expect to be at a non-smoking table: they don't exist.

Note: Most Vietnamese women don't drink or smoke in public.

3 Basics for the Business Traveler

Language

The national language, Vietnamese, is closely related to southern Chinese, but has romanized script. It is an easy language to learn, but hard to speak because it has six tonal sounds, meaning that one word can have six different meanings depending on the way it is pronounced. To make it even more difficult, the north and the south pronounce words differently.

> **Tip:** Many Vietnamese business partners provide their own interpreters. This is not always to your advantage. Bring your own or make a quick check to make sure the interpreter has a good knowledge and understanding of your language.

English and French are spoken as second languages. Generally the older people speak some

French and the younger people speak some English. Interpreters are available through tourist agencies or through investment service organizations.

Climate

The south of Vietnam has a tropical monsoon climate with the rainy season from May to November. The average temperatures are 25°C to 32°C (77°F to 90°F). In the hottest season (March, April, and May), Saigon can reach 39°C (102°F), and in the coolest month, the low is 21°C (68°F). The most pleasant time to visit Saigon is from November to January.

The north has a definite summer and winter, being subtropical with an extremely hot, rainy season lasting from May to November. November to January is the cool winter season. Winter daytime lows can fall to 13°C (55°F).

June, July, and August are the hottest months and temperatures can reach 33°C (91°F) in Hanoi.

In the north, the most pleasant months are between September and December.

Vietnam's humidity varies from 80% to 100%, making the hot seem hotter. It receives approximately 600 billion tons of rainfall each year. Northern and central highland temperatures are cooler than the coastal areas. Dalat's average annual temperature is 19.4°C (58°F).

What to Wear

Lightweight, breathable, western-style suits and dresses are appropriate for business and formal social occasions in Saigon all year around and in the summer in Hanoi. In the summer, it is very hot and short-sleeved business shirts with a tie are acceptable.

Never wear shorts. Tourists can get away with wearing shorts, but such attire will ruin a business-person's reputation. As a rule, it is best to dress formally for your first meeting. You may take off your suit jacket during this meeting. For future meetings, follow you host's mode of dress.

Heavier clothing, such as sweaters and wind-breakers, are appropriate to wear in the winter in the north. Temperatures can drop to 8°C (46°F) at night.

Dress is semiformal for most other occasions. A shirt and tie without the jacket is appropriate for men; women can wear skirts and blouses. Women should never wear anything revealing.

Tip: Dress casually for your arrival, both for comfort and so the touts will leave you alone. (Touts are paid a commission to lead you to particular shops or hotels, and they gravitate to people who they believe have more money.)

Note of interest: Although it is not acceptable for foreign women to wear anything revealing, it is interesting that the national dress for Vietnamese women can be just that. The *ao dai*, a form-fitting overdress with side slits to the waist and flowing pants is often made from silk so fine that it is see-through.

Visas

You must obtain a visa before entering Vietnam. Applications for a visa can be made at your nearest Vietnamese embassy or arranged through a travel agency.

All visitors must register an application inside Vietnam with the immigration authorities, which means through a registered travel company within Vietnam or with an external business travel agent. Because of internal communication difficulties, it is highly recommended that you use an external travel agent. This will make your life a lot easier. Call your Vietnam consulate for the name of a travel agent in your city who can arrange visas.

You may apply for different types of visas. If you are a first-time visitor who is just interested in checking out opportunities, get a tourist visa, valid for one month and available through a travel agent.

If you are traveling on business, arrange for a business visa, which is good for one month and extendible in Vietnam for up to six months, with multiple-entry facility. Business travelers who are working on foreign investment policies will be given visas that include permission to work. Business visas can be obtained on arrival at Ho Chi Minh City and Hanoi airports only if arranged in advance.

Allow two to three days for processing. To obtain a business visa you must have a letter from a local sponsor, a completed visa form, and four photos. Then it must be authorized by the Vietnamese Foreign Ministry.

> **Tip:** If you intend to arrive at one airport and leave from a different airport, make sure your visa specifies both cities or you may have to pay a local tax.

Multiple entry visas are available for regular visitors. They last three to 12 months and allow visitors to depart and enter Vietnam whenever the visitor chooses. This type of visa is difficult to get.

Visa extensions can be obtained from any travel company in Vietnam for a fee of approximately U.S. $25.

> **Tip:** Bring four extra passport-size pictures with you because you may be asked to fill out a second form. If you forget, as we once did, you'll be sent to the camera operator who will take your picture with an instant Polaroid. Then you'll wait in line a second time and have to pay for two pictures of yourself looking tired and jetlagged.

Health Matters

No particular health documents are required for travel to Vietnam, but local foreign doctors recommend you be inoculated against typhoid, tetanus, diphtheria, Japanese encephalitis, hepatitis A, and polio. Bring anti-malaria pills to use if you plan to travel outside major cities. Check with your local hospital's travel clinic for any new recommendations before you leave.

Bring any medication you may need. Although most prescription medicines are available over the counter, they are often called by different names. If you do need to buy any type of medication, go to a reputable pharmacy. On the black market you have no way of knowing the content and quality of medication. Some people stock up on medicine in Asia because some types can be quite cheap.

If you get any sort of cut or scrape, make sure antiseptic cream is applied at once. Germs breed faster in the humid heat than they would elsewhere. Infections often come on quickly, even in the big cities.

Tip: Drink only boiled or bottled water in Vietnam.

Two firms, International SOS Assistance and AEA (Asia Emergency Assistance), are planning internationally funded and operated clinics for foreigners in Ho Chi Minh City. An AEA emergency facility is open in Vung Tau.

Medevac coverage can be purchased from AEA International, Tel: 298520 (Saigon). The cost is approximately U.S. $400 per year for the resident abroad program.

International SOS Assistance can be contacted in Hanoi at 226228, and in Saigon at 242866. The cost is approximately U.S. $200 per year for membership.

Tip: In Vietnam, AIDS is known by its French acronym, SIDA. In April 1994, Saigon alone reported 110 new cases of AIDS.

What to Bring

Take along extra passport-size photos, batteries, and transparency/slide film (print film and good color processing is available everywhere.) Don't forget your corporate brochures. A money belt is a good safety precaution and very handy.

Remember that gifts are appreciated. Women's fashion magazines are good gifts for hotel staff and secretaries and will assure you tip-top treatment from them.

Business Hours

Most offices, including government offices, are open 8:00 a.m. to 4:30 p.m., Monday to Saturday. Lunch is generally from noon to 1:00 p.m., but a noon-time rest from the heat makes the lunch hour stretch from 11:30 a.m. to 2:00 p.m. Shops stay open until late in the evening. Restaurants, karaoke, and dance halls close around 11:00 p.m. Hotel discos and western-style bars stay open late.

Currency and Credit Cards

The basic unit of currency is the dong. Banknotes come in denominations of 100, 200, 500, 1,000, 2,000, 5,000, 10,000, 20,000, 50,000, half-million, and one million dong. Coins do not exist.

At the time of writing, U.S. $1 was equal to 10,500 dong, but recent trends have seen the number of dong per dollar come down. Obviously, check with your bank before you go.

U.S. dollars are the currency of choice in Vietnam and you will usually receive a fair rate of exchange. Unfortunately, however, when you spend U.S. dollars, you will receive dong as change. (U.S. coins are not accepted.) Try not to accumulate too much dong as it is impossible to exchange it upon leaving the country.

Note: The Vietnamese government plans to gradually end the use of the U.S. dollar in the country and to allow trade only in dong.

American credit cards are accepted now that the embargo has been lifted, but when you're away from hotels and large establishments, you will need cash. Vietnam is still a cash society. Cash advances from credit cards can be obtained from banks, but you will have to pay a commission.

Exchanging Your Money

You'll find the best exchange rates at banks, not money changers, and definitely not in hotels. Don't change money on the black market no matter how rewarding it may be. Authorities frown on travelers who trade on the black market.

Vietcombank outlets are located nationwide. Bring all your identity documents to change money.

Tip: Avoid changing too much money at once, or you will have thick wads of dong bulging in your pocket, making you a target for thieves. When you do change money, keep small bills for cyclo rides and other street purchases.

Tipping

Tipping is not expected, but is much appreciated. In the countryside and with cyclo drivers, boat drivers, taxi drivers, and others who go out of their way to help, a cigarette, cold drink, or small tip is appreciated.

Be aware that in hotels there is government tax plus service tax charged.

Bargaining

Bargaining is expected everywhere except in hotels, restaurants, department stores, and metered taxis. Learn what things are worth and be aware that the starting price for foreigners can be ten times or more above the real price.

Try to keep your bargaining good-natured. Test the merchants by pretending you don't want the item very much and walk away. If you are not called back with a final offer, you'll either have to pay their price or go away without it.

Making Phone Calls

All the new hotels have international direct dialing facilities, but international calls are very expensive. There are now telephone booths in Ho Chi Minh City, and phone cards are sold nearby. Paging services and mobile phones are also available.

> **Tip:** If you make a call from a post office, the clerk will take your passport while you make your call and then give it back when you have paid.

The price of sending a fax averages U.S. $7 per page to the United States. Hotels sometimes charge for receiving a fax on your behalf.

Telephone Area Codes

- Country code: 84
- Saigon city code: 8
- Hanoi city code: 42
- Haiphong city code: 312
- Da Nang city code: 512
- Hue city code: 54

> **Tip:** Always check areas codes with the operator. We have found that they are subject to change.

Note: If you are using a Saigon telephone directory that is older than 1994, you will see a 2 before each of the codes listed above.

Electricity

All new hotels have 110-volt power supply, with adapters available at the front desk. In older buildings, the power supply is anything you can imagine. It can be 110 and 220 volts, or 50 cycles or AC. Two-pin plugs are usual, but you'll also find flat-pin and round-pin ones. If in doubt, take an adapter.

Time Zones

Vietnamese time is GMT plus seven hours. There are no time changes across the country.

Holidays

Holidays and festivals are important in all Asian countries. It is wise to check ahead and avoid major holidays if you are intent on doing business. Offices are closed on holidays. All Sundays are holidays.

- New Years Day — January 1
- Tet (Lunar New Year) — January/February
- South Vietnam Liberation Day — April 30
- Labor Day — May 1
- Ho Chi Minh's Birthday — May 19
- National Day — September 2

Some unofficial holidays and festivals:

- Easter — March/April

- Buddha's Birthday — Usually early in May
- Chinese mid-autumn festival — September/October
- Christmas — December 25

Tip: Tet is not a good time to do business in Vietnam. The Tet is a three-day holiday, but private and government business slows down for the week before and the week after Tet.

News Media

There are radio stations in Vietnamese, English, French, and Chinese. The *Saigon Echo* is the French newspaper. Street vendors and hotel shops sell foreign and Vietnam-published papers.

A few hotels have satellite TV and some have in-house movies. English-language satellite stations including CNN World News, BBC World Service, Star TV, and a movie and entertainment channel are sometimes available.

English-Language Papers

It is possible to obtain English papers (e.g., the *International Express*) at hotels. The only daily Vietnamese paper in English is the *Saigon Newsreader*. There are various other publications published in English, including the quarterly *Vietnam Foreign Trade*, the monthly *Vietnam Courier*, and the weekly *Saigon Times*.

Business magazines of note are *Vietnam Today*, *The Vietnam Investment Review*, and *Vietnam Economic Times*.

> **Note of interest:** Censorship of local news by the government is practiced and penalties are imposed. However, *Vietnam Today* claims to be an independent publication. Vietnam's watchdog agency for foreign investment, the State Committee for Cooperation and Investment, publishes the *Vietnam Investment Review*. Sanctions are imposed on soft pornography or anything that glorifies or promotes the western way of life.

Airlines

Garuda, MAS, KLM, Cathay Pacific, Air France, Air Vietnam, Thai Air, etc. operate daily flights to and from Ho Chi Minh City and Hanoi from Asia, Europe, Australia, and the United States.

If you leave from the United States, one of the world's largest employee-owned airlines, United, flies directly to Vietnam. United also has an excellent network to most other Asian capitals.

If you are leaving from Vancouver, Canada, Cathay Pacific is a good choice, especially if you'd like to see Hong Kong on the way.

KLM may be the best bet for European travelers, because it departs from Amsterdam and other European hubs.

If you are taking a holiday with your trip, check Thai Air and fly Bangkok, then Phuket, or to the gorgeous island of Koh Samui, before or after Vietnam. Also check United.

Probably the most exotic location for a holiday and a spot of shopping is Bali. Garuda is the perfect choice; it often has good deals and is a safe carrier that often uses Australian-trained pilots.

The national carrier Vietnam Airlines also has a good schedule of domestic and international flights. They are upgrading, have hot meal service, and new aircraft. In 1994, they announced plans for a U.S. one billion dollar fleet modernization and expansion program. They also announced cooperative agreements with Delta, United, and Continental Airlines. Vietnam Air has direct flights to Australia, Singapore, Kuala Lumpur, Manila, Japan, Hong Kong, China, Bangkok, Moscow, Frankfurt, Amsterdam, and Paris.

Always make air reservations well in advance. Flights to and from Vietnam as well as domestic routes are usually very busy.

4 An Expedient Arrival

Planning Your Arrival

Saigon and Hanoi can be really hot in June, July, and August. Wear the lightest clothing possible for arrival so your body doesn't get too much of a shock. A short-sleeved shirt and light pants are good enough to get you to the hotel. Women can wear anything but shorts or sleeveless tops, which are considered inappropriate.

> **Tip:** If you are coming from a colder climate, take lighter clothes in your carry-on baggage so that you can change on the airplane.

Keep your suits for business, because if you look too well-heeled, you'll be swamped by people offering things you don't want.

If you arrive in the wet season, you will want an umbrella. (All the good hotels provide umbrellas for their guests.)

Arrival Forms

The flight attendants will provide you with your arrival forms to fill in, which include your baggage declaration form and an Application for Entry and Exit Note. Slip your forms into the picture page of your passport or international travel document, and keep your documents in your hand or somewhere easy to access.

Customs procedures are no laughing matter in Vietnam. When you fill in your arrival forms, do it correctly and make sure you do not misplace them when you exit the country.

On the entry-exit form, you need to attach a picture (which is why you should carry extras with you). Also, be sure to accurately describe your visa in the appropriate place. If you are on a business visa, check business. If you are on a tourist visa, check tourist. We were told by a consulate official that if you check a box that doesn't match your visa you could be harassed on the way out.

The baggage declaration form note must be filled out in duplicate, with the white top copy for customs and the yellow bottom for you to keep and then hand in when you leave the country. Make sure the writing comes through. Do not lose this copy! It is very time consuming for authorities to trace the top copy, plus you will be fined.

Turn this form over and you will see the heading "Pay Attention." You must declare foreign currency amounts over U.S. $3,000, plus any prohibited items. You are also meant to declare cameras, film, videotapes and video equipment, tape recorders, tapes, electronic items, etc. It is wise to prepare a list of serial numbers in advance. (**Note:** Taped videocassettes may be reviewed. Make sure there is nothing flagrantly western that has been slipped into your suitcase by mistake!)

Arrival

After disembarking the aircraft, you must stand and wait in the immigration queuing area. For the sake of expedience, make sure you stand in the correct line (foreign visa holder). Again, you'll be happier if you have changed into lighter clothes. Although the airport is modern and air-conditioned, it can still be hot and muggy (or cold and damp) in Hanoi.

Follow the sign to the baggage claim area. On the wall you'll see your flight number and carrier and the baggage carousel number. There are free luggage trolleys against the wall. It can take an inordinate amount of time before you see your luggage coming round. This is especially true in Hanoi and is probably partly because you and your luggage are bused in from the plane.

After picking up your baggage, you'll line up in one of the customs lanes in the customs hall. Look for the green "nothing to declare" exit for those who don't have dutiable items, but remember if you have more than 1.5 liters of brandy or over 200 cigarettes, you could be unlucky enough to be part of a random search and have your extra liquor confiscated. Always check customs regulations before you leave; they are subject to change.

> **Tip:** Remember you are in Vietnam. Showing anger at long lines, poor air-conditioning, no heat, or what you perceive as incompetence will get your luggage searched.

After you are through the customs hall, if you have arranged with your hotel for pick up, keep a sharp eye for someone standing in the crowd holding a sign with your name on it. If you have not prearranged pickup, go to the taxi stand; you'll see it as soon as you come out.

Note: In Hanoi, there are separate terminals for international and domestic travelers. Keep this in mind when you are leaving Hanoi. Noi Bai has been upgraded, but it still isn't up to the standard of Changi, or other Asian capitals. When you land in Hanoi, you will be bused to the airport building. Many of the buses in Vietnam are outdated and crowded.

Tip: Don't forget your duty free liquor and cigarette allotment. Even if you don't drink or smoke, you may want them for gifts.

Tip: There are foreign exchange booths at both airports, but you'll get a better rate of exchange at a bank in town.

Getting to the Hotel

Saigon

Tan Son Nhat International Airport is 7 km (4 mi.) from downtown Saigon, about a 15- to 20-minute trip. Vietnam Airlines provides a taxi service from the airport to the city for U.S. $10 to $15. Radio-metered taxi service is also available. Charges are reasonable: U.S. $7 to $10.

Your hotel can pre-book your airport transfer in a car for you. The cost on average is U.S. $15. Book when you reserve your room.

If you arrive in the early evening, especially on Sunday, you'll see a parade of young people on motorbikes, bicycles, and some cars going slowly around and around the downtown area. They start in front of the opera house at Lam Song Square, continue down Dong Khoi to the river, then up Nguyen Hue. This is the Vietnamese version of "cruising."

> **Note of interest:** In the late 1960s during the Vietnam War, Tan Son Nhat Airport was the busiest airport in the world.

Hanoi

Noi Bai Airport is 35 km (22 mi.) from Hanoi. Traveling time to the city usually takes an hour, and can take as long as one and a half hours, but will more likely take you one hour. (**Note:** A new highway is being built over the Red River which will eventually reduce the traveling time from the airport.)

Vietnam Airlines minibuses are available from Noi Bai to the city. This is the cheapest option, approximately U.S. $4 per person. Taxi fare is expensive at U.S. $25 to U.S. $35.

5 Highlights of the Major Cities

Saigon

Ho Chi Minh City, or Saigon as it is popularly called, is the economic center of Vietnam with a population of 4.5 million. Its French character has a particular charm.

Although Saigon is not the political or national seat of power, it is powerful because it is the economic capital. It is also a city that has maintained considerable autonomy by Vietnamese standards.

The city has never been able to shake the name Saigon and even airlines use that name on their baggage tags. In the 1950s, it was called the Pearl of Southeast Asia. Wealthy French colonials enjoyed a much more lavish life in Saigon than they could ever afford in Paris. The men were chauffeur-driven in lemon-colored Citroens, polished by their many servants. They threw dinner parties in their grand French houses. Caviar, French champagne, and cognac were served on gold-rimmed china and in

SAIGON
(HO CHI MINH CITY)

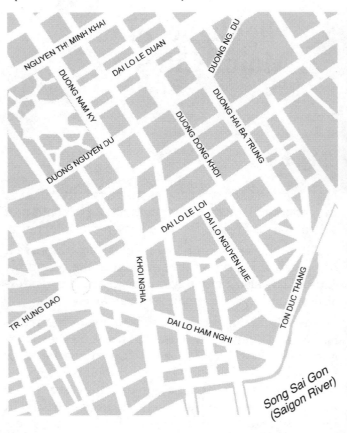

Song Sai Gon
(Saigon River)

fine crystal glasses under sparkling chandeliers. Everyone dressed to the hilt in the latest French evening styles and later they would dance the tango, with the patio doors open to let in the warm night. Wealthy Vietnamese were invited. Many had studied in France and knew the high life too. They copied the French style better than the French could. It is said that women who had both Vietnamese and French heritage were the most beautiful women in the world.

Then, during the Vietnam War, the city became a very dangerous, unpredictable place, yet it was still an elegant city with bright, neon-lit bars next to French bistro-style coffee houses.

Now Saigon is without question the hub of business and tourism; it is the ideal base for doing business and a fascinating place to be. The city has the character of a reckless teenager bent on wild times and the look of a grand old European lady who has been out of luck for awhile. You'll meet a lot of Australian, European, Asian, and American businesspeople in the hotels and restaurants. Saigon has the best places to stay and the best food.

Note of interest: Vietnamese reforms began here in the early 1980s. Communist party General Secretary Linh who lived and worked in Saigon was involved in the economic experiments of private capital zones.

What to Expect from Saigon

Saigon has always been more independent, innovative, and prosperous than her northern cousins. These characteristics have stymied Hanoi's efforts at state planning and have sometimes been a source of puzzlement and possible jealousy.

The Vietnamese are all rich in spirit, and you can especially feel this in Saigon. The people are unbelievably hardworking and helpful to foreigners. Think of the sight of a cyclo driver, peddling through the traffic and sometimes unbearable heat with a foreigner who weighs twice as much as he does. The driver, his arm outstretched to shield you from the traffic or tipping his carriage gently downwards so you can climb easily out, typifies the spirit of the South Vietnamese people — generous and appreciative.

For the first few days of your visit to Saigon, expect the unexpected. Remember that until recently and in some cases still, Vietnamese, especially those who worked for the Americans, were afraid to make contact with foreigners. But more likely than not, you'll be given a warm and generous reception from everyone you meet.

You will be asked personal questions by the Vietnamese, such as how old you are, where you are from, how much things cost, how much money you make, and so on. In Vietnam these questions are acceptable socially and are an indication of the Vietnamese interest in all things foreign.

Delays and red tape are part of life here, especially at the higher levels of bureaucracy. Even a little thing like extending your visa can be frustrating. Be patient and calm. A show of temper will set you back. If you are invited to sit, drink tea, and relax while you wait, then do just that.

In the evening, a nostalgic visit to pre-liberation restaurants and hotels is fascinating and you'll meet other businesspeople. If you want a city tour, look for "Du Lich," or tourist agencies. Any agency can arrange a tour.

Tip: New restaurants and bars are opening around Saigon. Be prepared to pay in Vietnamese dong because most don't accept credit cards. If you are caught short, they will happily change U.S. dollars for you at a decent rate of exchange.

Try Le P'tit Bistrot for wonderful French food. A genuine French chef from Lyon rules in the tiny, hot, but immaculate kitchen at 58 Le Thanh Ton, District 1 Tel: 230219. For lunch, a great pizza, or ice cream, trendy Vietnamese and a few foreigners eat at Ciao Cafe, 72 Nguyen Hue, District 1. And for the most wonderful Vietnamese food in an elegant atmosphere, try Lemon Grass, 63 Dong Khoi Street.

In the evenings, stop in for happy hour with a piano player at Vietnam House, 93 Dong Khoi Street, District 1. The Vietnamese food is also good.

Tiger Tavern, 227 Dong Khoi Street, District 1 is great for an after-work beer or lunch.

Q Bar, beside the National Theatre, is the hottest place for a late-night drink. David Jacobson designed it using all materials handmade in Vietnam. The result is wild!

Buffalo Blues, 72 A Nguyen Du, District 1, has jazz on some nights.

City Patterns

The city center, District 1, is small and well laid out, and street signs are easily seen. Nothing in the central business district seems too far away. Walking is a viable means of seeing the area if time permits and you don't mind the heat. Always check your map and consult your hotel concierge before you set out on foot.

District 1 is also the Central Business District (CBD) of Saigon. This area is bordered by the Saigon River and Le Duan Boulevard. Le Loi and Nguyen Hue Boulevard are at the central point. Most hotels, banks, and businesses are here.

Major boulevards and shopping streets are Nguyen Hue, Le Loi, and Dong Khoi. Most places are within a 20-minute walk.

The center, at Nguyen Hue Boulevard runs from the Saigon River to one block past the roundabout intersection of Le Loi. City Hall, a beautiful yellow, ornate landmark building, sits at the far end of Nguyen Hue. Dong Khoi is north of and runs parallel to Nguyen Hue.

Safety and Charity in Saigon

The Vietnamese are very honest, but in every society there is element of crime. With the recent surge of tourism and the hardships that have befallen the people in the past and the poverty they still face, it is not surprising that theft has increased.

Petty thievery does happen, but it is rare that there are serious crimes against tourists. Even so, don't go wandering around dark streets late at night.

> **Tip:** Do not wear gold jewelry, keep expensive pens in your pocket, or carry your valuables on your person. All hotels have either safety deposit boxes in the rooms or at the front desk. Use them!

The first few times you are out, you'll be approached by postcard, coin, and stamp sellers. These are usually sweet-looking children as young as five years old. This method of supporting themselves is better than begging, but be aware that a few of them are pickpockets.

The postcards (or other items) they sell are usually quite cheap, and if you make a purchase, they'll get to know you and leave you alone.

You'll always see sidewalk shoe shiners, coconut sellers, weighers, astrologers, and manicurists. Keep in mind that these people are trying to avoid begging for money.

The first time you leave your hotel in the evening, you'll see that the beggars have come out. Considering that the population of the city is over four million people, the number of beggars you see is minimal. Most only beg if they are truly incapacitated. You may want to keep small notes in your pocket to give to these unfortunate people.

Note of interest: Many times we passed the tiniest, oldest, strangest looking Vietnamese artist we'd ever seen. He was neatly dressed in beret and smock, trying to sell his watercolors on the boulevard. If we hadn't known better, we would have thought we were in Paris. When we stopped and admired his lovely watercolors, but said we didn't want to buy, he said, "Look, give me anything for one. It doesn't matter how little. I am starving!" When we gave him U.S. $4, he insisted on giving us a second painting of our choice as a gift.

Hanoi

Hanoi is situated on the right bank of the Red River, and is 70 km (43 mi.) from the Gulf of Tonkin. Since 1976, Hanoi has been the capital of the unified Socialist Republic of Vietnam. Between 1954 and 1976, it functioned as the capital of the Democratic Republic of North Vietnam. Almost three million people live in Hanoi, with a density of two people per square meter (two people per square yard).

During French colonial times, Hanoi was said to be one of the most beautiful cities in Asia. It now feels a bit like a has-been with a split personality. On the plus side, it has lovely tree-shaded streets, lakes, some French architecture, and pretty parks and squares. On the down side, it feels dirty and neglected. The neglected feeling comes from the fact that it has lost most of its talented people to Saigon. Even government officials would rather be in Saigon!

Tip: Hanoi does not have the selection of hotels and restaurants that Saigon has. Always book well in advance for your hotels. The best hotel in Hanoi is the Metropole on Ngo Quyen Street. It is a an old twenties-style building, close to the Municipal Theatre, that has been meticulously restored. The rooms are small, but this Sofitel, French-run hotel has everything.

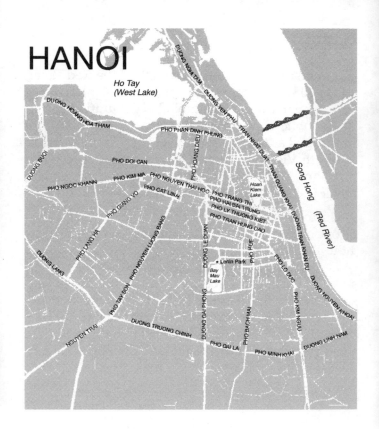

HANOI

Ho Tay
(West Lake)

DUONG NGHI TAM

DUONG YEN PHU

TRAN NHAT DUAT

DUONG HOANG HOA THAM

DUONG BUOI

PHO PHAN DINH PHUNG

PHO HOANG DIEU

PHO DOI CAN

PHO NGOC KHANH

PHO KIM MA

PHO NGUYEN TRAI HOC

PHO TRANG THI

PHO HAI BAI TRUNG

PHO LY THUONG KIET

PHO TRAN HUNG DAO

PHO CAT LINH

PHO GIANG VO

PHO NGUYEN LUONG BANG

DUONG LE DUAN

Hoan Kiem Lake

Song Hong (Red River)

TRAN QUANG KHAI

DUONG TRAN KHAN DU

PHO LANG HA

PHO TAY SON

PHO HUE

Lenin Park

Bay Mau Lake

PHO LO DUC

DUONG NGUYEN KHOAI

DUONG LANG

DUONG GAI PHONG

PHO KIM NGUU

NGUYEN TRAI

DUONG TRUONG CHINH

PHO DAI LA

PHO BACH MAI

PHO MINH KHAI

DUONG LINH NAM

Because it is what it is, a bureaucrat's city, Hanoi is fraught with red tape and endless waits. It is also, like Saigon, a walking city. Hanoi has benefited somewhat from market reform and an inevitable increase in construction.

City Patterns

Hanoi has four districts or *quan.* The central district (Hoan Kiem District) is south and west of Hoan Kiem Lake. Streets are usually shady and cool.

It is bordered by the Red River (Song Hong) to the east, with the Chuong Duong Bridge leading into the Ancient or Old Quarter that sits at the top of this district.

Note of interest: Hanoi was first called Thang Long or Soaring Dragon. When the city was built under the Later Le Dynasty, it was planned to have harmonic balance. The city center was placed at a point believed to be at a line of communication with the center of the earth. Important buildings covering religion and administration were built in the north, south, and east of the center, according to each building's function. The ancient configuration of Hanoi has been almost obscured by war, colonialism, and natural disaster.

Hotels and airline offices and businesses congregate south of the lake, on Trang Thi Street, Ba Trung, and Thuong Kiet. These streets runs east and west on the south side of the lake.

Tourism offices and embassies center around Quang Trung. This street runs south from Hoan Kiem Lake.

Northwest of Hoan Kiem Lake is the Ancient Quarter of 36 Streets. This is the shopping area. Hang Gai Street specializes in silk clothes and lace tablecloths, napkins, and sheets. As well, tailor-made suits and jackets are available in 48 hours here. Silk, jade jewelry, and oriental rugs are also worth buying.

Tip: In the Ancient Quarter, the street names are representative of what is made and sold on the streets. *Pho* means passageway or street.

The French Quarter, located near the central district, is north of Bay Mau Lake and west of Hoan Kiem Lake.

This newer urban section of Hanoi is opposite the French Quarter, in the southwest quadrant. Lenin Park is at its center.

6 Getting Around with Ease

Both Hanoi and Saigon are good "walking cities." Check with the concierge at the front desk of your hotel before you set out for directions; if you have the time and don't mind the heat, foot travel may be the best way to go.

Cyclos

The cyclo is the traditional Vietnamese taxi. It is a three-wheeled pedicab peddled from behind by a stalwart, hardworking Vietnamese male or, less often, an older female. Riding in a cylo is a fun, cheap way to travel for a short distance. No visitor to Vietnam should go home without having ridden in one.

Cyclos are practical as one-seaters for western-size people. The seats are leather and can get warm, but if the sun shines too brightly you can ask the driver to put up the hood.

Settle on a price before you get in. Also write down the address you want to go to and show it to your driver before you start out. Drivers may pretend they know what you want when they don't have a clue.

> **Tip:** In Saigon to travel one way anywhere within the central business district will not cost more than 5,000 dong.

Hire your favorite driver for the day. He'll peddle you anywhere and will wait patiently for you to return. If you choose one who speaks your language, you will likely have an interesting tour. You'll find the majority happy, helpful, caring for your safety, and even loyal. A day's services should cost U.S. $5 to U.S. $10, depending on the distance.

If you are on a short mission, the driver will be happy to wait. Arrange this in advance and expect to pay more than a one-way fare. Also expect to pay more late at night, and when it rains.

Note of interest: It costs a cyclo driver U.S. $150 to buy the rights to a pedicab, which is beyond the means of many. Don't be put off by their aggressiveness in trying to get you to take a ride. They are only trying to make a living and it's not an easy one.

There have been reports of late night drivers asking for more money than was agreed upon when you arrive at your destination. Before you get in, count the agreed upon amount in front of him.

Tip: Although cyclos are a practical alternative to walking, remember that they are not allowed on some streets, so their routes may be longer than what you can cover on foot.

Taxis

Taxis in Vietnam cannot be hailed on the street. You must have the front desk of your hotel call (or you can call yourself) a cab or call the metered radio dispatch service.

In Saigon, call Vinacab on 442170, Airport Taxi 444466, or Saigon Taxi 297545 in Saigon.

In Hanoi, call Hanoi Taxi on 265252 or Thang Long Taxi 265241.

Note: Check these numbers when you get there; they are liable to change.

Most taxis have meters. Make sure your driver turns it on. If there is no meter, either find out how much it should cost or get another cab. One half-hour ride, covering approximately 10 km (6 mi.) should cost approximately U.S. $10.

> **Tip:** Taxi fare is high within the city and availability can be sporadic. Plan in advance. Have your hotel desk call for short-run taxis. Otherwise book in advance for a half-day or day trip.

Motorbikes

You will likely be approached by men with motorbikes wanting to take you on a tour. A half day on the back of a motorbike will cost around U.S. $10. Have a chat to make sure that they are suitable tour guides.

If you are visiting over the long term, you can rent a Honda or bicycle from MOLO, in the Opera House across from the Continental. Or ask at your hotel. Hondas cost U.S. $8 to U.S. $10 per day.

Buses

Buses are not suitable for business travelers. They are cheap but uncomfortable. The wooden benches of these old buses only provide leg room for people shorter than 5' 5".

Car Rentals

If you have a day-trip planned, it is advisable to hire a car with a driver. Cars with drivers can be hired for the day or by the hour, or you can hire a minivan with driver.

All hotels plus travel agencies provide this service. Prices are standardized.

Tip: A time saver if you have to sit in traffic in a rental car is a rented mobile phone. Rather than wasting time, you can make business calls to arrange tomorrow's appointments, discuss tactics with your partners, or whatever. Cell phones are also an alternative to businesspeople setting up offices, since the wait for telephone installation can be up to three months or longer. Ask your hotel business center if they offer phone rentals.

There are very few cars in Vietnam, and at the time of writing, it is not possible to rent a car to drive yourself, even for trips outside the city. If you do want to travel outside the city, you can arrange to rent a car with a driver, but be sure to meet with the driver first and check that he or she is suitable. For example, you want to be sure that the driver's command of English will get you through a couple of days on the road.

Trains

The trains in Vietnam are slow. They run from Ho Chi Minh City, stopping at Da Nang, Nha Trang, and Hue and arrive in Hanoi two to three days later. The faster train is known as the "Special" express. Trains are the most comfortable type of land transport Vietnam has to offer, but as a foreigner, you will pay up to eight times more than a Vietnamese.

There are also daily trains from Hanoi to Haiphong which take only a couple of hours.

Train trips must be booked at least one day in advance. Book first class; economy class provides only a wooden bench.

Saigon Station (Ga Sai Gon) — Tel: 45584

Hanoi Station (Ga Ha Noi) — Tel: 52628

Hydrofoil Service to Vung Tau

The daily hydrofoil service to Vung Tau leaves the waterfront close by the Majestic Hotel in Saigon at 8:00 a.m. and takes one hour and 20 minutes. It leaves Vung Tau for the return journey to Saigon at 4:00 p.m. There is bar service onboard. Tickets are available from 66 Hoang Dien, District 4.

Airline Travel

Until recently, Vietnam Airlines (Hang Khong Viet Nam) had a very bad safety reputation, and business-people that needed to fly between Hanoi and Saigon would actually fly out of Vietnam to Bangkok and then take Air France or Thai Air back to either Saigon or Hanoi. Part of the reason for the poor safety record was the lack of spare parts. This situation is rapidly changing.

Now Vietnam Airlines has a good schedule of domestic flights on some new aircraft. In 1994, they announced plans for a U.S. $1 billion fleet modernization and expansion program and announced cooperative agreements with Delta, United, and Continental Airlines.

7 An Economic Overview for Business

In 1986, The Sixth Party Congress of the Communist Party of Vietnam realized the only way the country could survive was to deregulate the economy. This landmark decision opened the door for foreign investors to establish business and joint venture activities in Vietnam.

The Sixth Congress of 1986 introduced the "economic renovation" and ended the country's attempt at a central planning system. Many economic errors had been made between 1976 and 1986 when the north and south were reunited. The Sixth Congress attempted to correct these errors and set the country on track by moving away from a centrally planned economy to a multi-sector, free-market-oriented economy. (It is the government's objective to increase its gross domestic product (GDP) to 9% by the year 2000. This did not look attainable until the U.S. embargo was lifted in 1994.)

Investors in Vietnam were initially hesitant. They were fearful of losing their assets to the government, being unable to repatriate profits, and the potential delays caused by a Communist-based bureaucracy. Since deregulation, the Vietnamese government has tried to assure investors they have no need for such concerns.

The Law on Foreign Investment (FIL) originally enacted in 1987, continues to be amended. Many businesspeople consider FIL to be far from perfect, but workable. Amendments affecting areas such as foreign exchange control, accounting procedure, and land usage are frequently made. Further laws were passed in 1992 to strengthen certain economic rights, including protection for foreign investors against nationalization of their assets.

> **Tip:** While assessing your involvement in Vietnam, be sure that any advice and information you receive is based on the most recent interpretation of new legislation and amendments to FIL.

Because of the country's history, having been influenced by the French, Russians, and Americans, Vietnam's legal system can seem confusing to investors. The Vietnamese government is in the process of streamlining its legal process for everyone's benefit. They are particularly emphasizing matters relating to business development, trade, and incentives for foreign investors.

Inflation

Inflation wreaked havoc on the economy at the end of the 1980s, reaching a peak of 400% and dropping to 80% at the end of 1991. During the balance of the 1990s, inflation is estimated to average in the high-single or low-double digits.

Debt

In early 1994, the Paris Club of Western Creditor Nations accepted a rescheduling of Vietnam's foreign debt. Eleven countries agreed to cancel up to 50% of Vietnam's debt payment. At that time the country's foreign debt was U.S. $4.5 billion.

Average Income

Vietnam has one of the lowest per capita income levels in the world. The average annual income for the Vietnamese worker is U.S. $200 per annum. For employees of foreign controlled companies, there is a minimum monthly wage of U.S. $35.

Vietnam offers a type of old age security through a payroll plan. The government requires that employers pay 10% of their payroll and employees pay 10% of their earnings into the plan.

Employment

Vietnamese are industrious and respected for being able to quickly learn and apply new technical skills. Nearly 75% of the population are educated in secondary schools, colleges, and universities. Foreign investors need look no further than Vietnam to find industrious and skilled workers at a low labor cost. (**Note:** the minimum working age is 18, although 16-year-olds may be hired as trainees with the permission of their parents.)

The restructuring of government enterprises, reduction in armed forces, and other factors caused the unemployment rate to climb as high as 20% during the mid-1990s. The total work force exceeds 30 million with 72% in agriculture, 21% in industry, and approximately 7% in service-related industries.

Tip: Japanese firms in the metallurgy and foundry industries will be moving as much as 20% of their casting production to Southeast Asia. Vietnam has a good source of silica sand and a strong work force and is expected to attract more than its share of this industry, although the work force is inexperienced at this type of work. It is believed that with the help of expatriate specialists, local technicians can quickly improve their skills.

Local experts believe that 35% of agricultural output is produced by the most primitive means. This would explain why agriculture represents less than 32% of the GDP. The industrial sector represents 20%, and service industries 48% of the GDP.

Hiring foreign specialists is often required, due to the lack of local expertise in certain industries. The government may insist that a company establish a training facility for Vietnamese workers so they can eventually replace foreign specialists.

Note: Vietnamese citizens must be given priority for all jobs.

Tip: Foreign owners of local enterprises must learn patience and tact when managing Vietnamese workers. Misunderstandings often occur when Western management styles clash with the culture and language differences of Vietnam. The Vietnam Arbitration Organization is referred to in any employer-employee dispute that cannot be settled by the parties involved. Employment in certain occupations, such as domestic staff, must be handled through a government agency.

Infrastructure

Regardless of what emerging country you think of, infrastructure offers the biggest opportunity, and Vietnam is no exception. The government realizes the need to improve roads, bridges, ports, power facilities, telecommunications, and tourism facilities. In its desire to create a modern infrastructure, the government is receptive to proposals from foreign companies with expertise in these particular fields.

> **Note of interest:** Vietnam and the Canadian province of Quebec have established a number of joint ventures. One project includes construction of a U.S. $12 million traffic control system between Saigon Port and Vung Tau. Montreal-based Tanbers Co. and Pha Ruang Ship Building built a U.S. $2.5 million ship repair factory.

Telephone installations in Vietnam doubled from 42,690 in 1992 to 86,000 in 1993 and the number of telephone subscribers doubled from 150,000 in 1991 to 300,000 in 1993. The number of telephones per 100 people has increased from 0.26 per hundred in 1992 to one per 100 hundred in 1994.

These numbers fit the pattern of telecommunications as one of the fastest-growing industries in emerging countries. The number of telephones per 1,000 people increased 150% from 1965 to 1991 in emerging countries, compared to an increase of only 41% in developed countries.

The construction industry of Vietnam has always been important to the economy. An example of one joint venture involved businesspeople from Singapore, Macau, Hong Kong, Taiwan, China, and South Africa. The Singapore company in the joint venture was to be granted a license to build infrastructure facilities in the Export Processing Zone of Haiphong in north Vietnam. The syndicate will invest U.S. $150 million to develop a 300-hectare (741-acre) site of warehouses and factories to be leased out to foreign manufacturers. It also plans to construct 1,000 apartments, 600 deluxe townhouses, 600 luxury holiday villas, a golf course and other recreational facilities. The total project may end up using 1,000 hectares (2,471 acres).

Tip: The Asian Development Bank on occasion provides grants to research infrastructure developments. They provided U.S. $1 million to study the feasibility of the creation of a transport corridor through Laos, Thailand, and Vietnam. Once completed, they will be seeking proposals and tenders.

Cement companies are often very successful due to the amount of building and road construction. Esso Singapore opened a representative office in Hanoi and Saigon to introduce their asphalt products. Petrolimex Saigon and Esso will jointly market three new kinds of asphalt, anti-sinking, enhanced sticking, and recyclable.

Tip: There are a total of 105,600 km (65,630 mi.) of roads in Vietnam. Only 13,000 are paved, 92,600 are gravel or earth. Bridge construction and renovation is a big priority. Heavy trucks cannot cross one-third of the country's 8,200 bridges. The Ministry of Transport and Communications has set up a special department, the Project Management Unit, to handle proposals and tenders from foreign companies wanting contracts in this lucrative area.

Vietnam also suffers from severe electricity shortages. The government is planning a U.S. $400 million upgrade in the transmission and distribution of power in Saigon. The investment required to modernize the country's electrical system is astronomical, but it has to be done. Power companies and consultants from around the world are trying to get a piece of this action.

Consumerism

The face of Vietnam is changing. The country may be one of the poorest in the world, but with new industries being developed, the middle and upper classes have increased their discretionary buying power and there is a growing demand for consumer-related products. The trendy Q Bar and Manhattan (Vietnam's first North American-style fast-food restaurant) are Saigon's way of catering to this new clientele. Kentucky Fried Chicken and Pizza Hut restaurants are opening. Pepsi is the fastest growing beverage in south Vietnam.

Note of interest: Pepsi's bottling plant in Saigon was opened just hours after the U.S. embargo was lifted. It produces 400,000 to 500,000 bottles a day. McDonald's, on the other hand, according to local experts has made a conscious decision not to enter Vietnam for a few years, and is concentrating instead on expanding its operations in China. This may give the other fast-food outlets a jump on McDonald's, or it may give "Ronald" time to find the right partner before making a commitment.

Consumer products ranging from reggae stores to pharmaceutical companies and fashion stores are already in demand from Vietnam's new middle class, who are starved for Western consumer products and services. Hanoi's first international standard supermarket opened in 1994. The 330-square meter (3,500-square feet) shop is a joint venture with Seiyu Ltd, a Japanese supermarket chain, the diversified Mitsubishi and the Vietnam National Agricultural Import-Export Corporation. Annual sales are expected to exceed U.S. $2 million.

Tip: Vietnam imports two million liters of water a year. With the increasing number of tourists and the new demand from locals, this is a growth business. There are at least 20 kinds of purified water, with two-thirds of them coming from other countries.

Between 1980 and 1992, the number of households in emerging countries, like Vietnam, that owned a television set increased 153% compared to an increase of only 21% in developed countries. Daewoo Corporation of South Korea and the Hanoi Electric Company (Hanel) established a joint venture in Vietnam and a second one with Hanel in 1994. Their U.S. $33 million project is to produce and sell refrigerators and electronic products, such as television sets, to the Vietnamese.

According to national statistics in Saigon, 64% of households have televisions, 24% refrigerators, 54% motorcycles, and 20% have VCRs. As wages rise, there will be increased spending in various areas. There has been a 17% rise in spending on consumer goods, a 27% increase in spending on culture and education, a 43% increase in spending on medicine, and a 49% increase in spending on transportation. Foreign investors don't fully appreciate consumers' increasing purchasing power, greater leisure time, and the size of the Vietnamese consumer market.

Manufacturing

Industry has changed considerably since the mid-1970s. Trade and company structures have been relaxed a great deal. State controlled or partially controlled businesses and industries are becoming more deregulated and less controlled. This has been necessary to allow the new multi-sector, free-market-oriented economy to work.

Foreign investment pledges for projects topped the U.S. $10 billion mark in September, 1994. This figure accounts for all projects since 1988 when the government opened the country for business. In 1994, 25% of total foreign investment came within nine months, from January to September.

The manufacturing sector in Vietnam is in its embryonic stage and Vietnam is ready for all types of industry. Practically all equipment and machinery is imported and spare parts are a rarity. Specialists in all areas are needed to help establish and effectively manage industries ranging from metallurgy to building supplies.

In 1993, the General Company for Cement Production imported 10,000 tonnes of manhedi-chromite fire-resistant bricks at a cost of U.S. $9 million. Demand is expected to increase to over 40,000 tonnes a year by the end of the decade. To meet this demand, a factory is being constructed with assistance from Magnensitwerk AkenGmHB, Laeis Bucher, and Mend Heim from Germany.

Vietnam's leather industry is also expanding. Ten industrial tanneries produce 7,000 to 8,000 tons of salted hides per year for the 300 or so handicraft establishments around the country. Leather exports, which include shoes, sandals, bags, and briefcases, have grown from U.S. $60 million per annum to almost U.S. $100 million in a couple of years.

The motor vehicle industry should expect incredible growth in the near future. The main method of transport is the motorcycle with few cars being available. Mercedes Benz, BMW, and Renault have plans to change this by doing joint ventures with the Vietnam Motor Corporation. The government has been encouraging foreign auto manufacturers to team up with local firms. Fiat has already established a bus and light-truck assembly plant.

Mining

There are extensive deposits of minerals ranging from bauxite and gold to iron ore and zinc. The country has substantial untapped deposits of natural gas and oil. Coal has been the number one energy source for the Vietnamese.

Coal mining was getting out of control with illegal mines being set up and coal sold through illegal channels circumventing the now-dissolved Vietnam General Corporation of Coal, which had been set up to regulate the industry. In 1994, the Prime Minister closed dozens of mines in an attempt to put illegal mines and wharves out of business.

> **Tip:** It is the government's objective to double annual coal production to 10 million tonnes by the year 2000. To achieve this target, coal experts believe that about 300 million cubic meters of earth need to be moved by the turn of the century at an estimated cost of U.S. $550 million.

Oil and Gas

Vietnam's natural resources are attracting foreign investors in droves. In 1994, 110,000 barrels of oil per day were being pumped out of the ground compared to only 20,000 a day in 1989. Their objective is 300,000 barrels a day by the year 2000. This will be achieved through joint ventures and will require foreign experts to advance the industry in areas of exploitation, processing, distribution, and import and export.

Vietnam's first refinery was a joint venture with France's Total Petroleum. The second is expected to be a joint venture with American Jobec Corporation and Canadian Saint Martino Inc. The refinery is to produce 130,000 barrels a day and will cost U.S. $1 billion.

Vietnam has extensive natural gas reserves and is just beginning to harness this power. The Vietnamese are looking forward to changing from cooking over coal and wood to natural gas. A new primary industry and service industry is being created by this switch from coal to natural gas to provide natural gas appliances.

In late 1994, South Korea's Hyundai Corp. finished installing a 283 km (175 mi.) gas pipeline connecting south Vietnam to the port of Vung Tau. An international syndicate of British Gas Plc, Mitsui & Co., and Trans Canada Pipeline are bidding on the next stage of development.

Tip: Local experts suggest the importance of natural gas is being ignored by foreign companies looking for a quicker return on crude oil.

Oil is the country's leading export, natural gas is being under-utilized. BP, Atlantic Richfield, and Mobil Corp. have all made substantial natural gas discoveries. In October 1994, British Petroleum (BP) announced a natural gas discovery in the Nam Con Son basin south east of Saigon. It was estimated to have recoverable reserves of two trillion cubic feet of gas. The equivalent in oil would be 350 million barrels.

Local consumption of liquefied petroleum gas (LPG) exceeds 5,500 tonnes a year. The Vietnam Petroleum Cooperation (Petrolimex) has set up joint ventures with a number of overseas firms including BP and Wesfarmers Kleenheat Gas Asia Ltd. of Australia. Wesfarmer is contributing 50% of the capital to import LPG and buy local gas, and bottle it for distribution locally. It is anticipated that the usage and demand for LPG is going to increase significantly. BP's project involves producing and marketing of lubricants.

With the U.S. embargo lifted, there will be no holding back major U.S. oil companies from participating in Vietnam's lucrative natural resources. This also creates opportunities for service industries to support new exploration companies.

Fishing

The Vietnamese have fished for centuries and have an abundance of marine life in their waters. Fishing territory ranges from the Gulf of Tonkin down the coast and around into the Gulf of Thailand.

In recent years, shrimp farms have moved their operations from Malaysia to Thailand and Indonesia. It is anticipated that Vietnam will become the preferred location to establish shrimp and other seafood farming projects. Vietnamese prawns are 3% to 5% cheaper than the closest competitor — Thailand.

> **Note of interest:** In August 1994, a trial shipment of 18 tons of frozen prawns was shipped for the first time to Florida in the United States. Canada buys U.S. $5 million a year of Vietnamese prawns. Until Vietnam can obtain Most Favored Nation status, exports to the United States will not be in large volume.

Agriculture

Vietnam has traditionally focused on agricultural production. Agriculture accounts for about 40% of GDP. Rice represents almost 60% of the total agricultural output. Approximately 85% of all cultivated land in Vietnam is used for rice production.

The country is trying to improve growing techniques by modernizing its methods and better utilizing natural resources. Opportunities exist for foreign investors experienced at cost-effectively increasing rice production or providing value-added benefits to rice growers.

The north is trying to develop its Red River delta to produce vegetables, fruits, and flowers for export. Contracts with the far eastern region of the Russian republic generated U.S. $15 million in 1994. The Vegetable and Fruit Corporation wants to turn this into a U.S. $50 million-a-year industry by the year 2000.

Two state-of-the-art dairies are being set up by an American businessman who has been following Vietnam's potential since 1989. The joint venture involves Vietnam's National Dairy Company (Vinamilk) and the U.S.-based Ashta International. Ashta will contribute U.S. $12 million to the U.S. $18 million venture. Two farms will be established, one in Ha Tay province in the north and the other just outside Saigon. Each farm will have approximately 2,000 head of cattle.

Export-Import

Historically, state-run businesses controlled trade in Vietnam. Now the private sector is catching up. The new level of competition and the need for profitability gives the private sector a big advantage and trade opportunities exist in every industry sector within Vietnam.

Watch out for trade deals involving the government when they try to settle their foreign accounts through third-party arrangements. For instance, if another country is in a deficit position to Vietnam, the government can assign the debt owed Vietnam to the foreign business. Then the onus is on the foreign investor to collect from the other country's government.

Tip: When establishing a trade relationship, either with a Vietnamese customer or a potential partner, make sure you know what the other party's financial position really is and that this person has the authority to do business with you. Vietnamese businesses wanting to conduct trade with foreign partners must deposit a sum of money with the Ministry of Commerce and Trade before they are duly authorized. The amount, in U.S. funds, will depend on the type of trade they wish to handle.

It is wise for foreign suppliers to ask their local buyers for an advance cash payment, or at least a meaningful deposit. Letters of credit are becoming more often used. Vietnamese banks try to make sure lines of credit are supported by the appropriate amount of foreign currency.

The Vietnamese Chamber of Commerce and the Ministry of Commerce and Tourism can confirm whether the Vietnamese buyer or potential partner you may be considering is authorized and able to do business with you.

Vietnam's major trading partners have been Japan, Hong Kong, Singapore, and the former Soviet Union. Major imports include consumer goods, heavy equipment, fertilizers, and petroleum products. Major exports are rice, seafood, and natural resources such as forest and mineral products.

Also affecting trade in the near future will be Vietnam's success or failure to join the Association of Southeast Asian Nations (ASEAN). Vietnam has tried to join ASEAN through the Treaty of Amity and Cooperation in Southeast Asia. It is anticipated that the application will be approved in the short term, unlike Myanmar, Cambodia, and Papua New Guinea, whose applications have been declined. The member countries are Indonesia, Brunei, Malaysia, Thailand, the Philippines, and Singapore.

In 1992 ASEAN formed AFTA, the ASEAN Free Trade Area. Its objective is to open the doors of trade among these six countries and 340 million people. The average growth rate for these country's economies is 6% with a total GDP of $430 billion. Tariffs on as much as 85% of goods traded within ASEAN members are to drop to between 0% and 5% by the year 2003.

The ASEAN countries make up an important part of the membership of the Asia Pacific Economic Cooperation (APEC). APEC takes the concept of free trade agreements to the ultimate. It connects the whole world, with the exception of the European community. APEC is comprised of Australia, New Zealand, China, Japan, Hong Kong, Taiwan, South Korea, the United States, Canada, Mexico, Papua New Guinea, Chile, and the six ASEAN countries.

One of Vietnam's major problems in its trade dealings is that it is not one of the 114 members of the Uruguay Round of the General Agreement on Tariffs and Trade (GATT). Nor does it appear that Vietnam will become a member by 1995 and benefit from favorable reciprocally reduced tariffs. Vietnam also does not have Most Favored Nation (MFN) status with the United States. This means that tariffs on Vietnamese footwear products are 35% compared to 6% for MFNs; certain wrist watches could pay a 6.25% tariff, but Vietnamese imports must pay an 80% tariff. The tariff on cotton apparel goes from 10% to 90%. There will also be a ceiling on the amount of imports allowed into the United States from non-MFN countries.

Tourism

Vietnam welcomes one million tourists a year and expects this figure to increase substantially before the turn of the century. The government encourages tourism development, and in 1994 there was more investment by foreigners in hotels and tourism than any other sector of the economy other than general industry. Oil and gas was a close third.

Anticipating increased tourism, Vietnam Railways upgraded its version of the Orient Express. A 1,000-mile track running from north to south will give tourists the opportunity to see the country, making as many stops as they like. Foreign investors initiated the idea. The British-based Orient Express is expected to operate the service.

According to local reports, gambling is being introduced by Stanley Ho's Macau group. The Do Son resort, 15 km (9 mi.) south of Haiphong, has always been a favorite holiday spot for residents of Hanoi, including the last emperor Bao Dai. It will now cater to international tourists.

The 600-room New World Hotel in Saigon opened in 1994 as Vietnam's largest hotel. Hotel construction in Saigon is big. In the next few years many hotel groups will have new hotels in Vietnam including Delta, Ramada, Capital Hotel (Hong Kong group), Saigon-Elysees Hotel, and Malaysia's Noi Bai Golf Resort. Hanoi hopes to have between 8,000 and 10,000 international standard hotel rooms by 1996. That's a big increase from 1994 when there were only 500 international standard rooms.

International airlines are gearing up for the increased demand by tourists for flights to Vietnam. Vietnam Airlines may increase its fleet to as many as 80 aircraft in the next 15 years. This pleases Boeing immeasurably, since they have been exploring opportunities in Vietnam since 1992. Local industry experts suggest Vietnam Airlines could grow to be the size of Thai Air or Cathay Pacific over the next 20 years.

Vietnam Airlines is working with a number of different airlines around the world. Cargolux, a Luxembourg freight group, is developing air freight in

Europe with Vietnam Airlines. Region Air, a new group out of Singapore, provides aircraft and crews.

> **Tip:** Foreign passenger, freight, and courier airline companies should give serious consideration to strategic alliances with Vietnam Airlines and other tourism or transport companies.

8 Joint Ventures and Doing Your Business

Foreign Investment Law and Business Structures

The Foreign Investment Law (FIL) dictates how business may be conducted in Vietnam. There are basically four structures in which foreign investors may establish their ventures. **Please note:** The following explanation is only an overview of the laws at the time of writing. Before proceeding too far with a venture, ensure that you obtain qualified advice from local experts in Vietnam.

The State Committee for Cooperation and Investment (SCCI) is the government body that vets all investment applications and issues approved companies with an investment license. The investment license will state exactly what your business activity is allowed to be. It is advisable to keep SCCI informed of the progress of your initial and ongoing negotiations. Keeping SCCI fully informed may assist in expediting the application process. Starting in 1995, all business enterprises have to present environmental impact assessments before an investment license can be granted.

Business Cooperation Contracts

A Business Cooperation Contract (BCC) is a contract between a foreign investor and a Vietnamese party to undertake a project. These cooperative ventures are the most flexible and provide the least amount of government intervention.

Unlike the other three options (described below), a BCC does not create a legal entity, but does state the respective benefits and responsibilities of the parties involved. These contracts must obtain approval and a license from the State Committee for Cooperation and Investment (SCCI) before any business activities can go forward.

A BCC application should include the proposed contract, a report on the technical and economic feasibility of the project, and all necessary and relevant information that could possibly relate to the venture. This will help expedite the process. The SCCI will determine what is necessary, so to speed up the process it is better to provide as much information as possible up front.

Any changes to beneficial ownership or rights and responsibilities of a BCC requires the approval of the SCCI and the respective parties.

Joint Venture Enterprise

Joint venture enterprises are possibly the most practical method of doing business in Vietnam. The government prefers these structures. A good Vietnamese partner can assist you with the SCCI and help you adjust to language and cultural barriers while fast-tracking your manufacturing and distribution.

However, finding the right partner is not always easy. In fact, local experts suggest that having the wrong partner is infinitely worse than having no partner.

A joint venture agreement is established between a foreign investor and a local Vietnamese party. The local party could be a medium-to-large Vietnamese company or government entity. The foreign partner must invest a minimum of 30% of total equity.

100% Foreign-Owned Enterprises

Foreign-owned enterprises are businesses that are established with 100% foreign capital. They are known as limited liability companies. They are unable to use public financing or trade their shares freely. They are usually the preferred structure for most foreign businesses as it gives them the greatest freedom and control over their own project.

However, the government tries to discourage these enterprises and prefers to have local companies involved and learning from foreign experts. If the project is important to the growth of the country, such as infrastructure, or is to be situated in a region like Central Vietnam, there is greater likelihood of obtaining SCCI approval.

> **Note of interest:** Accounting firms are setting a precedent by establishing 100% foreign-owned companies. Deloitte Touche Tohmatsu was the first. Ernst & Young, Price Waterhouse, and KPMG Hungerford were next in line with Coopers & Lybrand and PKF close behind.

The SCCI has the authority to close down or liquidate 100% foreign-owned projects if they breach any Vietnamese laws or the conditions and terms of their investment license. Remember, you are a guest in their country; play by their rules or prepare for the consequences.

Build, Operate, and Transfer Contracts

Build, operate, and transfer contracts are between a foreign company and a Vietnamese government entity. They are highly effective contracts that allow infrastructure construction to be completed at a minimal cost to the government. The foreign company agrees to build and operate some needed infrastructure, such as a toll-highway or port, and then transfer ownership back to the government. The transfer to the government occurs after an agreed-upon duration (and profit-making period for the foreign investor). The foreign partner, and usually their subcontractors, will be entitled to preferred tax rates or tax holidays.

> **Tip:** Infrastructure construction is a big opportunity in all emerging countries. Vietnam is considered by some to be pre-emerging and may present the greatest opportunity anywhere for foreign investors with expertise in infrastructure development.

Terms and Conditions

When establishing any type of project in Vietnam, foreign investors must comply with prevailing rules and regulations. Here are some of them in summary, but always check with experts before you get in too deep:

- The foreign party must contribute a minimum 30% of the total equity of the project. There is no maximum limit.

- Terms of a business cooperation contract or joint venture agreement can be any duration up to 50 years (15 to 30 years is more common), with most able to be extended.

- All foreign-owned or partly foreign-owned projects must comply with Vietnamese accounting practices. All projects must have two bank accounts: one for foreign currency and the other for Vietnamese dong. Accounting records and ledgers must be kept in local currency and in the local Vietnamese language.

Tip: Apply to the State Committee for Cooperation and Investment for their approval to maintain company records in another language and currency. They will probably approve as long as records are still maintained in local currency and language.

- The Ministry of Finance insists an audit is conducted each year. In 1994, audit rules were relaxed allowing foreign investors to appoint their own independent accountancy firm. This freedom is limited to 100% foreign-owned, limited companies, joint stock companies, and international agencies, but does not include joint ventures.

- Foreign investors are encouraged to develop projects in certain industries while being restricted from others. The Foreign Investment Law prioritizes industries that will assist the long-term development of Vietnam. Special benefits or incentives for these prioritized industries include a reduced tax rate in the vicinity of 15% to 20%. Normal tax rates are 20% to 25%. To obtain further incentives, the project should have a minimum capitalization of U.S. $10 million, with 80% of production exported or generating 80% of its revenue in foreign currency. If a project does not earn excessive profits compared to similar projects and if it is located in an unfavorable region, foreign investors may qualify for further incentives.

Note: Projects that increase export production or reduce the need for imports, infrastructural projects, and any business that earns foreign exchange, such as tourism, are encouraged by the government. Industries that help raise the technical and skill level of local workers, or industries that rely on local labor and raw materials are also encouraged.

Representative Office

Representative offices do not need approval from the SCCI as they are not considered an investment. Representative offices can be very useful in arranging contacts and contracts for your company's head office. They are effective ways of introducing your company to the business community, government officials and the public in general.

According to regulations, the purpose of a representative office is to aid the implementation of an investment project and not to conduct any trade with Vietnamese individuals or companies. The Minister of Trade and Tourism regulates representative offices and to obtain your license you must locate the office that handles your country within the ministry. In principle, the Ministry of Trade is supposed to notify the applicant within 60 days of receiving an application for a representative office.

Licenses are issued for three years. If you operate with an expired license, be prepared for a fine of up to U.S. $20,000. For operating without a license or illegally doing business, you will be kicked out of the country and fined U.S. $50,000.

Take along an interpreter to prevent any misunderstandings. The application process tends to get bogged down, so in order to expedite matters, it is advisable to remain in the country while your application is being processed. It is a good idea to appoint an experienced lawyer or accountant to help speed up the system.

Setting up an Office

Real estate prices are unbelievably expensive in downtown Saigon, and so are telecommunications. It is also difficult to find a good location. Saigon is not a city with abundant space. There are renovations by foreign companies of old colonial buildings going on everywhere because just about everything needs major refurbishing. Even new buildings need work before they are livable. Prices for office space and expatriate accommodation are just as expensive as Hong Kong and Singapore. There is much talk of them going through the roof.

The experience of setting up in Vietnam requires four luxuries: patience, time, dedication, and money. However, the rewards to be reaped make it all worthwhile. Remember, there is a consumer market of seven to ten million in Saigon and Hanoi alone. Your rewards will not only be financial ones.

Tip: Many businesspeople start by setting up a short-term office in a hotel. This is a convenient but obviously expensive option. The costs of setting up office telecommunications systems are also unbelievably high. Local phone installation can cost about U.S. $1000, and only if it doesn't include wire replacement. The time between application and installation can be up to three months and longer.

There are many agencies cashing in on the high demand for office space and rental. The Saigon Business Centre rents furnished short- and long-term office space and communications systems. It also has business support services. Contact the Centre at —

Saigon Business Centre
49-57 Dong Du Street
District 1 Ho Chi Minh City
Tel: (84)8298777
Fax: (84)8298155

Export Processing Zones

Export Processing Zones (EPZ) are designated areas where businesses are established to benefit from preferential customs duties. Several zones have been established and new ones are being designated. Two of the larger ones are Tan Thuan EPZ near Saigon and the Danang EPZ in Central Vietnam.

The mandate for an EPZ is to provide low labor costs, political and social stability, tax preferential treatment, good access to seaports and airports, stable power and water supply, efficient telecommunications, support to service industries in the vicinity, access to spare parts, a simple application process with minimum bureaucracy, and a comfortable living environment for expatriates. Many EPZs in Southeast Asia have failed by not providing this needed infrastructure. It is hoped that Vietnam's will succeed where others have failed.

If your project involves manufacturing, you will have a four-year, tax-free holiday after your first year of profitability. After that a 10% profit tax will be imposed.

Service companies will get a two-year tax holiday once they become profitable following which they will incur a 15% profit tax. They will also be entitled to tax credits for three years or more for profits reinvested, a 5% tax on repatriated profits, duty free import of all machines and equipment, and duty free export of finished goods.

The Local Partner

The local partner may contribute to a partnership in anything from local currency, technology, labor, building services, or natural resources. The local partner could be a private individual, company, or a non-resident Vietnamese. State enterprises and joint state-private enterprises can also be local partners. Government economic entities may not be local partners.

The Foreign Partner

Foreign investors bring the all-important foreign exchange to a business relationship. They will also bring technology, and whatever equipment, tools, and appliances are required for the project.

Foreign investors are not allowed to buy land in Vietnam that is owned by the public. However, they can lease land or property for business purposes.

The law surrounding foreigners buying land in Vietnam is continually changing, so be sure to obtain a legal interpretation of the most recent rulings. And watch out for Tax Decree #60-CP, which implies a forced sale for foreigners who leave the country;

foreigners leaving the country have only 90 days to sell or they will forfeit their house.

Note: Vietnamese rules and regulations change with the growth of the country. It is the intention of the government not to put foreign investors at a disadvantage when laws change. Article 99 in the FIL allows the SCCI a certain flexibility to protect foreign investors should laws change and be retroactive. The SCCI is allowed to change the objects of your enterprise and license. It can reduce or grant exemptions from tax to offset any disadvantages caused by changes in the law.

Tip: Use a consultant who is up to date on all regulations. Have an experienced lawyer scrutinize your contracts, with particular emphasis on clauses relating to *force majeure* termination and changes in economic circumstances.

Helpful Government and Private Agencies

Check all addresses and telephone numbers before you go — things are always changing.

State Committee for Co-operation and Investment (SCCI)

This is the central authority that approves all foreign investment.

178 Nguyen Dinh Chieu Street
District 3
Ho Chi Minh City
Tel: 294674

Chamber of Commerce

Helpful for finding suitable trade and joint venture partners.

171 Vo Thi Sau, Ho Chi Minh City
Tel: 230598

Export Development Trading Corporation (EDTC)

The first non-government officially approved international buying agent in Vietnam. They have smaller offices in Hanoi.

6 Dong Khoi Street
District 1, Ho Chi Minh City
Tel: (848)296448
Fax: (848)296454

Foreign Trade & Investment Development Centre of Ho Chi Minh City (FTDC)

City agency promoting foreign trade and development. Provides information on foreign trade, investment, and economic law. Also organizes trade promotions and offers business and secretarial services.

Main office at 92-96 Nguyen Hue Avenue
District 1, Ho Chi Minh City
Tel: (848)222982
Fax: (848)222983

Services of Foreign Economic Relations

45/47 Ben Chuong Duong, Ho Chi Minh City
Tel: 292911/298116

Chor Pee & Company

The Colonade, 27 Nguyen Trung Truc
District 1, Ho Chi Minh City
Tel: (848)224986
Fax: (848)225441

9 Banks, Investments, and Financial Services Opportunities

Banking

Vietnam's banking and investment industry is changing daily. Traditionally, there has been a mistrust of banks in Vietnam. People believe it is safer to keep their money under the bed than in a bank. The government is trying to change this belief.

At last count, there were about 30 foreign bank representative offices and three joint venture banks from Indonesia, Malaysia, and South Korea. Citibank was the first American bank to apply for a branch operation. Bank of America was expected to be next in line.

At the time of writing, there were nine foreign banks with branch licenses. The major ones include Banque Indosuez, Banque Nationale de Paris, Bangkok Bank, Australia New Zealand Bank, Standard Chartered, and Credit Lyonnais, which is the only one with branches in both Hanoi and Saigon.

In view of the immaturity of the market, the representative offices are probably the most cost efficient way of operating. Some institutions realize the length of time it will take to become a profitable branch and are in no hurry to set up an operation.

Banking and investment regulations change regularly. At the time of writing, the Vietnamese government had just allowed foreigners to buy shares in any commercial bank with a prescribed minimum capital of U.S. $5 million and one or more years of profitable operation. Foreigners are not allowed to own more than 30% of the prescribed capital.

Banking Activities

The main activities that foreign banks are allowed to conduct include cash operations in Vietnamese dong and U.S. dollars. They are also allowed to handle transactions in the currency of their home country. For example, The Bangkok Bank is only allowed to trade in dong, U.S. dollars, and Thai baht.

Foreign banks may conduct domestic and international fund transfers. Corporate current accounts, fixed deposits, and certain foreign exchange transactions can be provided. They can arrange international trade financing and provide working capital or investment financing. Trade and investment advisory services and the issuing of contract bonds and guarantees can also be provided by foreign bank branches.

Capital Requirements

Banks require U.S. $10 million capital before they will be considered for a banking license. All banking license applications have to be approved by the Governor of the State Bank. Many of the laws relating to finance are unclear, and often non-existent, so foreign financial institutions should tread slowly. At present, there is no mortgage law, which makes foreign lenders a little nervous. (A mortgage law is expected to be passed in the near future.) There were also no laws governing capital markets at the time of writing and this had not been prioritized.

Securities Market

The Vietnamese investment and securities market is just being born. There is talk that a stock market will be set up in Saigon in 1995.

Tip: Brokerage houses should set up representative offices and position themselves for the eventual opening of a stock exchange. The government will need outside consultants to advise on its structure. Opportunities abound for companies familiar with the setup of stock exchanges. This includes brokerage and investment houses and companies that produce stock-trading software.

Note of interest: It may take a while for the HCMC (Ho Chi Minh City) exchange to get up and running. According to an interview in the Vietnam Economic Times with the State Bank Governor, Cao Sy Kiem, there are three conditions that must be met before the government can consider establishing a stock market: a range of companies owned by both private and joint stock companies, a securities and exchange law, and a stock exchange organization. None of these existed at the time of writing.

Investment Services

Investment services provided by the banks are very basic and don't get much more creative than fixed-term deposits.

In 1994, banks introduced products to attract money that normally never found its way off the street. These life insurance type products being sold through the banking system were intended to attract 800 billion dong in 1994 and as much as 1,200 billion dong in 1995.

Tip: Financial institutions and investment houses able to offer a range of services and be patient during these "pre-emerging" years will reap the dividends in time to come.

Mutual Funds

Closed-End Funds

A closed-end mutual fund is one where the manager issues a fixed number of shares that are traded on a stock exchange. This differs from an open-ended fund (see below) where the manager will buy back shares from investors at their net asset value.

There are a couple of closed-end funds of particular interest. The Vietnam Frontier Fund (VFF) listed in 1994 on the Irish Stock Exchange was a U.S. $50 million fully subscribed float. The fund will trade over the counter through securities dealers in London. The official selling agents for the fund are Japan's Nomura Securities, and HG Asia Ltd., an affiliate of U.S.-based Smith Barney Shearson. The fund manager has a very impressive list of shareholders including Yoshihisa Tabuchii, former president of Nomura Securities; Tony Lowrie, Chairman of HG Asia; Stephen Swift, Chairman of Global Asset Management for Credit Suisse; and William Colby, retired director of the U.S. Central Intelligence Agency during the Nixon administration.

The fund's objective is to create a diversified investment portfolio in different parts of the country. Investing in different sectors of the economy, this fund will provide an investor with exposure to natural resources, banking and financial services, infrastructure development, consumer products, real estate development, manufacturing, and more.

The fund is, in effect, providing much needed venture capital to approved companies. The VFF will take an active role in the development of local companies it invests in. The fund hopes to bridge some of the problems new companies have in raising capital from traditional lenders.

Three other closed-end funds have approximately U.S. $170 million under management. They are Beta Vietnam Fund, Keppel Vietnam Management Pte. Ltd., and Vietnam Management Co. On the New York stock exchange, Templeton Management Ltd. listed a Vietnam fund during 1995.

Open-Ended Funds

The world's emerging markets are attracting more and more investor attention. In recent years, the average economic growth of emerging markets has been two to three times that of developed nations. Vietnam, considered by some to be a pre-emerging nation, presents potentially even greater returns for investors.

Investors and fund managers are watching with great interest the birth of the stock exchange in HCMC.

Note: Direct share investment in stock markets of emerging countries can be difficult for non-residents because of the time delays in buy and sell orders. Obtaining qualified and up-to-date research can also be very difficult.

If you are an investor who wants a share in the exciting growth of these stock markets, you should use Hong Kong or Singapore registered unit trusts or open-ended mutual funds registered in your home country and managed by experienced money managers.

> **Tip:** Diversifying investments into a number of emerging countries through a Southeast Asian Regional Fund managed by an experienced money manager can substantially reduce the risk of being exposed to just one individual market. Tiger or Dragon Funds (Southeast Asian Regional funds) can provide substantial returns to investors. There are a number of top quality fund managers based in Hong Kong, Singapore, Kuala Lumpur, and Jakarta managing regional and individual country funds.

Exceptional returns are due in part to high savings and investment rates that support long-term economic growth. Younger demographics, increased consumer spending, and a low-cost and highly productive labor force also play an important role in the foundation of their sustainable growth.

Jardine Fleming Unit Trusts registered in Hong Kong offer individual country funds, including Malaysia, Korea, and Hong Kong, plus regional funds. Jardine Fleming manages one-third of the Canadian Global Strategy's Asia Fund along with Rothschild and AsiaInvest.

Thorntons (a member of the Dresdner Bank Group) is based in Hong Kong and offers a range of Tiger and Dragon Regional Funds. Single country funds for Thailand, Malaysia, Indonesia, Singapore, and others are also available. Thorntons manages the Universal Far East Fund for the Canadian group Mackenzie. Asset allocation of the fund is based on Thorntons' Little Dragons Fund.

Nomura Securities, one of the world's largest investment companies, has offices around the world and is strategically located in Asia. They manage a wide range of regional and single country funds. In Canada, their expert money management can be obtained by investing in AGF Japanese and Asian mutual funds.

Note of interest: Sir John Templeton pioneered the concept of investing in emerging markets. For decades his team has scoured the world looking for companies that represent good value and excellent potential. Available in most western countries are Templeton Emerging Market Funds, which traditionally have been top performers.

Tip: You can invest in some of Templeton's listed emerging market mutual funds and specialized funds such as their Vietnam fund on the New York Stock Exchange. For Templeton's open-ended mutual funds, contact a trusted and experienced mutual fund broker.

Insurance

Vietnam's insurance industry has, until recently, been controlled by the government-owned company Bao Viet. Private insurers are now allowed to offer a wide range of personal and commercial lines of insurance.

Foreign insurers are not rushing to set up offices until a proper and enforceable insurance law is written. In the meantime, it is anticipated that major international insurers will set up representative offices and be ready for approaching opportunity.

Companies will be able to operate as a joint venture, a branch of a foreign insurer, a 100% foreign-owned company, or have a shareholding in local private or state-owned insurers. Wholly foreign owned insurers will need capital of U.S. $5 million. Joint ventures or Vietnamese private insurers will only need 20 billion dong (U.S. $1.85 million).

Establishing a brokerage will require less capital and is probably less risky until insurance law is finalized. The prescribed capital for a foreign-owned brokerage is U.S. $300,000.

The Finance Ministry is solely responsible for issuing licenses as well as regulating the industry.

Health Insurance

Expatriates doing business in Vietnam all have one bit of advice in the event of illness or serious accident: go to Hong Kong or Singapore. Corporate health insurance products are becoming more common in salary packages for middle and senior management, but the main feature of health insurance is to evacuate the insured for medical treatment to Singapore or Hong Kong in the event of a serious illness or an accident.

Asia Emergency Assistance and SOS are two of the main providers of evacuation insurance. Foreign health insurance underwriters will be watching the Vietnamese market as insurance law becomes more defined. Corporate employee benefits will eventually be a lucrative market.

10 Best Buys: Saigon and Hanoi

Various shopping opportunities exist in Vietnam, and when you are shopping, remember that you can bargain for almost everything. If you don't bargain, you are paying too much.

Shopkeepers will change your U.S. dollars for you at a pretty fair rate of exchange. Small shops won't take credit cards.

Tip: Buyer beware! Many antiques are good fakes, so know your market.

Saigon

Dong Khoi Street, District 1, between Le Loi Boulevard and Ton Duc Thang Street, is the main shopping street. You'll find silk, clothing, lacquerware, wood carvings, art galleries, antiques, and everything else there.

Paintings and art are available at many galleries. Try Art Gallery Saigon, 57 Nguyen Du Street, District 1. The owner guarantees that each work is an original.

Art Gallery Particullier, 43 Dong Khoi Street, District 1, has a private exhibit of famous Vietnamese artists. Oils, watercolors, gouache, and paintings on silk are available here.

You'll find that for painting, Hanoi is the main art center, Saigon comes next. Original paintings by a new artist may cost upwards of U.S. $100. Already famous artists command up to U.S.$ 1,000. Deceased artists' work goes for more. Buy direct from the artist and you'll save money.

Silk and embroidery is available at Viet Silk at No. 43 Dong Khoi Street, District 1. They have a wholesale factory that takes orders in Danang. Vu Ban Quang on 76 Le Thanh Ton Street, District 1, also has silk and embroidery for export.

Bamboo, shell, and beaded wall-coverings painted with Vietnamese designs can be found at Shop Anh Tuyet, 30 Nguyen Hue Street, District 1. They will make to order. A hanging the size of a door costs U.S. $8 to U.S. $10.

Lacquerware, sometimes with mother-of-pearl inlay, is a bargain in Saigon. It is made from a resin extracted from the son tree. Furniture and large vases are available from Lam Son Company, 106 Nguyen Van Troi, Phu Nhuan, across from the Omni Saigon Hotel.

Tip: Copycat Zippo lighters with various inscriptions from the Vietnam war are available on street corners. Computer software is available at the Ben Thanh Market.

Hanoi

Handicrafts, including lacquerware, are available in the shops on Hang Khay and Trang Tien Streets, south of Hoan Kiem Lake.

Silk can be found on Luong Van Can Street, and you can get it tailored on Hang Gai.

Brass Buddhas and other figures are available in Ngu Xa, old Hanoi. These craftsmen have been famous for their brass work since the middle of the eighteenth century.

Ceramics can be bought at the village of Bat Trang, 10 km (6 mi.) southeast of Hanoi.

Shipping

It is much more convenient to ship your goods home. Lep International Freight Forwarding has an office in the Mondial Office Building at 203 Dong Khoi Street, District 1, Tel: (848)242000 Fax: (848)243405

11 Where to Stay

Quality hotels are not cheap in Vietnam. Saigon should get cheaper soon with the rash of new hotels that are opening. Both a Delta and a Ramada are set to open in 1996. Hanoi has a poorer selection of hotels.

Prices range from U.S. $50 for a small room at the boutique hotel, Mondial, to U.S. $500 for a suite in one of the five-star foreign or joint-venture-owned establishments. Other than in the five-star hotels, don't expect the same standard as you get in other countries.

Hotel Listings

Hotels that we specially recommend are noted in boldface below. Five-star accommodation have all facilities and are noted (*****). The inexpensive range is U.S. $50 to U.S. $70; moderate hotels charge approximately U.S. $70 to U.S. $90 for a simple room; and expensive ranges from U.S. $100 to U.S. $200 per standard room and up to U.S. $800 for a suite. It is worthwhile to upgrade to at least a moderately priced room.

Hotels charge a 10% government tax plus a 5% to 15% service charge needs to be added to the prices. (Unless otherwise noted, prices are in U.S. dollars.)

Note: There is a law in force that is meant to curb prostitution. The law states that Vietnamese of either sex are not allowed in a foreigner's hotel room while guests are present. Hotel staff are forced to police this law. To avoid embarrassment for your Vietnamese guests, ask them to wait in the lobby or bar.

Saigon

Century Saigon   **Recommended*****
Nguyen Hue Boulevard
Tel: (848)23818
Fax: (848)292732

A suite costs $95 to $350. New, modern, 100-room hotel located on the main street. Among savvy business travelers to Saigon, the Century has the reputation as the best business hotel. It is classified as a boutique hotel. The rooms are very small, but elegant and comfortable. Ask for a deluxe room; the difference is a window you can open so you can keep an eye on Saigon and to breathe the still-fresh nighttime air. The marble lobby bar is an all-day and evening meeting place for businesspeople and deals are made over its tables. The location can't be beat. Includes two restaurants, business center, health club, and in-house movies.

The Saigon Floating Hotel   *****
Hero Square
Tel: (848)290783
Fax: (848)290784
Tel: 1-800-835-7742 or 1-800-441-3847 for reservations.

An expensive, small-roomed but pleasant hotel, an-
chored on the river. The first to have western standards.
This hotel originally started out on the Great Barrier
Reef but was bought by the Vietnamese government
and towed in 1989 to its current position beside a small
compound with a pool and tennis courts. The river
views are fascinating. The hotel has two restaurants,
three bars, disco, business center, and a fitness center
run by Southern Pacific Hotels Corporation.

Omni Saigon   *****
Nguyen Van Troi Street
Tel: (848)449222
Fax: (848)449222

Very expensive. A new, larger hotel with 250 rooms.
Located in the Phu Nhuan district of town, 15 minutes
from downtown and ten minutes from the airport.
Business center, grand ballroom. Rooms are spacious
and have satellite TV and in-house movies. There is a
desk in each room. Outdoor pool, health club, sauna,
gym. Executive floor offers complimentary breakfast
and lounge for a more expensive rate. The hotel is
beautiful but the location is too far from the center of
Saigon. They have a free air shuttle bus that drops
you off and picks you up across from the Century
Hotel. If time is not a concern, and you don't mind
the shuttle ride, it's a good bet.

The Landmark Serviced Apartments and Offices   *****
5B Ton Duc Thang
District 1
Tel: (848)222098
Fax: (848)222110

Serviced studio, one-, and two-bedroom apartments. All amenities including health club. Rents from $2,900 per month, minimum stay one month.

The Continental   Recommended****
Dong Khoi Street
Tel: (848)299201/3/6
Fax: (848)290936

Moderately priced. City center and the nicest of the old hotels. A spacious French colonial style building, predating the war but since renovated. Former hangout of Graham Greene and Somerset Maugham. The lobby bar is a great place to sit after a hard day's work and look out over the busy main square. The Italian restaurant, Guido's, is in a fabulous French Renaissance room and the service is good.

The Mondial   ****
109 Dong Khoi Street
Tel: (848)296291/296296/296273
Fax: (848)296324

Inexpensive, small, 40-room boutique hotel with good location and good value. In-house movies, mini bar, 24-hour room service. Upgrade if you can!

The Rex   ****

Nguyen Hue Boulevard
Tel: (848)292185 or (848)293115
Fax: (848)296536 or (848)291469

Moderate to expensive. Renovated, historic hotel in
city center, run by Saigon Tourist. Business center,
office space for foreign companies, and room safes.
Upgrade to a junior suite or higher if possible. The
roof terrace is recommended.

The Cuu Long (Majestic)   ****

Dong Khoi Street
Tel: (848)295515
Fax: (848)291470

City center, overlooking the river. If you book here, try
to get the piano suite overlooking the river. The hotel
underwent renovations in 1994.

Saigon Weekend Ideas

> **Tip:** Don't miss a day trip to the infamous
> Cu Chi Tunnels. They are located in Cu
> Chi, 35 km (21 mi.) northwest of Saigon on
> the road to Tay Ninh.

Tip: If you are a runner, meet the Hash House Harriers, a group of expats that have formed a joggers' social club. They invite both businesspeople and tourists to jog, chat, and have a drink with them. Meet at the Saigon Floating Hotel at 3:15 p.m. on Sundays. Please check the time in advance because it could change. Small donation of U.S. $5 is required.

Vung Tau is a popular weekend beach destination for the Saigonese, just 178 km (110 mi.) southeast of Saigon. It used to be popular with the Russians who were looking for oil off the coast. Before that it was R & R for the GIs during the Vietnam War. The daily hydrofoil service to Vung Tau leaves the waterfront close by the Majestic Hotel at 8:00 a.m., and takes one hour and 20 minutes. It leaves Vung Tau for the return journey to Saigon at 4:00 p.m. There is bar service onboard. Tickets are available from 66 Hoang Dien, District 4.

Learn scuba diving with a NAUI instructor or cruise and snorkel or dive from the junk, Song Sai Gon, along the beautiful Nha Trang coast in the South China Sea. A two-day, two-night cruise including meals costs U.S. $400 per person (not including transportation to Nha Trang). Contact the Scuba Diving Centre, with an office at 17 Pham Ngoc Thac, District 3, HCMC Tel: (848)296750, Fax: (848)231591, or in Nha Trang at Cau Da Village, Tel: 01(58)23966.

Hanoi

There are very few hotels in Hanoi, but there are new ones opening up each month. Hotels are far superior in Saigon, but Hanoi is catching up. Book early because there are few hotels and even fewer that meet western standards.

Pullman Sofitel Metropole   **Recommended*******
15 Ngo Quyen Street
Tel: (844)266919
Fax: (844)266920

Expensive. The best hotel at the moment. Good location in the central district. Beautifully restored 1920s-style building. All services and facilities expected from a western hotel, but the rooms are smaller. Business center, outdoor pool, in-house video, French Brasserie, drycleaning, and airport shuttle.

Hanoi Hotel   ****
D8 Giang Vo Street, Ba Binh District
Tel: (844)252240
Fax: (844)266631

Expensive Chinese/Vietnamese joint venture hotel with good reputation. Restaurant, nightclub, karaoke, and business center.

Heritage   ***
Giang Vo
Tel: (844)344727
Fax: (844)343882

Expensive. Coffee house and swimming pool. Try to upgrade.

Thang Loi   ***
Yen Phu Street
Tel: (844)268211
Fax: (844)52800

Moderate. Restaurant, disco, swimming pool, and tennis court.

Sun   ***
Mai Hac De Hanoi
Tel: (844)253916

Inexpensive. A small hotel with good management. Ten minutes from the city center. Satellite TV, air-conditioning, and fridge in each room. Book early and try to get the best room.

Military Guesthouse   **
33 Pham Ngu Lao Street
Central
Tel: (844)232528
Fax: (844)267424

Inexpensive.

Hanoi Weekend Ideas

> **Tip:** If you are a runner, meet the Hash House Harriers, a group of expats that have formed a joggers social club. They invite both businesspeople and tourists to jog, chat, and have a drink with them. They meet on Saturdays at 4:00 p.m. at various locations. A flyer is available at the Metropole Hotel, Sunset Pub, Lan Anh bar, and Club Opera. Small donation of U.S. $5 is required.

Do Son, an ocean destination that can be a respite from Hanoi's summer heat, was a favorite retreat of Vietnam's last emperor, Bao Dai. A three-hour drive from Hanoi, Do Son is 18 km (11 mi.) south of Haiphong. Although the beaches are not great, find "beach number three" for some tranquil, simple solitude. This area has been marked for future resort development by a Hong Kong firm. It is also famous for its seafood.

Seafood restaurants are located along with karaoke bars on the promenade behind beach one and two. Accommodation is rundown, but the guest houses that were formally old French-colonial-style villas are right on the beach.

There is also a small hotel, The Hai Au Hotel, Tel: 01(31)61221. No beach, austere atmosphere, satellite TV, U.S. $25 to U.S. $40. Reservations needed during July and August.

Recommended Reading

Travel — Probably the most literary travel book available on Vietnam is *Introduction To Vietnam,* by Jacques Nepote and Xavier Guillaume (1992, Odyssey, Hong Kong). It has fascinating and illuminating excerpts from historical interviews.

The Maverick Guide To Vietnam, Laos and Cambodia, by Len Rutledge (1994, Pelican Publishing Company, Gretna, Louisiana) is wellset out and has a lot of useful travel information.

History — Stanley Karnow's *Vietnam: A History* (1983, Viking Press, New York) is well worth a read to understand Vietnam's turbulent history. This book is meant to be a companion to the PBS documentary "Vietnam: A Television History."

For an understanding of communism in Vietnam, Ho Chi Minh's *Selected Works* (1962, Foreign Languages Publishing House, Hanoi) will prove illuminating.

There are some very good books that deal with the Vietnam War. These include James Fenton's *All the Wrong Places* (1988, Atlantic Monthly Press, New

York) and Australian journalist Frank Palmos's *Ridding the Devils* (1990, Bantam, New York).

Literature — Graham Greene's *The Quiet American* (1955, Penguin Books, London) is required reading for those interested in fiction.

Norman Lewis's *A Dragon Apparent* (1951, Scribner, New York) is a travel book written in 1951 about pre-war Vietnam.